Gun Control in Germany 1928-1945

William L. Pierce

NATIONAL VANGUARD BOOKS

ISBN 0-937944-07-6

PUBLISHED BY NATIONAL VANGUARD BOOKS
POB 330 • HILLSBORO • WV 24946

PRINTED IN THE UNITED STAES OF AMERICA

Gun Control in Germany, 1928-1945

by William L. Pierce

A common belief among defenders of the Second Amendment to the U.S. Constitution is that the National Socialist government of Germany under Adolf Hitler did not permit the private ownership of firearms. Totalitarian governments, they have been taught in their high school civics classes, do not trust their citizens and do not dare permit them to keep firearms. Thus, one often hears the statement, "You know, the first thing the Nazis did when they came to power was outlaw firearms," or, "The first thing Hitler did in Germany was round up all the guns."

One can understand why many American gun owners *want* to believe this. They see in the current effort of their own government to take away their right to keep and bear arms a limitation of an essential element of their freedom and a move toward tyranny, and they want to characterize the gun-grabbers in the most negative way they can. Adolf Hitler has been vilified continuously for the past 60 years or so by the mass media in America, and certainly no politician or officeholder wants to be compared with him. If the gun-confiscation effort can be portrayed convincingly as something of which Hitler would have approved, it will have been effectively tarred.

This identification of the inclination to deny citizens the right to keep and bear arms with National Socialism and Adolf Hitler has been strengthened recently by clever magazine advertisements which show Hitler with his arm outstretched in a Roman salute under a heading: "All in favor of gun control raise your right hand." A Jewish group, Jews for the Preservation of Firearms Ownership (JPFO), quite noisy for its size, has been especially zealous in promoting the idea that the current gun-control effort in America has its roots in Germany during the Hitler period. This group has gone so far as to claim in several articles published in popular magazines read by firearms enthusiasts that the current restrictive legislation being proposed by the U.S. government is modeled on a gun-control statute enacted by Germany's National Socialist government: the German Weapons Law (*Waffengesetz*) of March 18, 1938.

Again, one can understand the motivation of the JPFO. Many non-Jewish firearms owners are well aware that the movement to restrict their rights is led and promoted primarily by Jews, and anti-Jewish feeling has been growing among them. They know that the controlled news media, which are almost unanimously in favor of abridging or abolishing the Second Amendment, are very much under the influence of Jews, and they know that the most vocal anti-gun legislators in the Congress also are Jews. It is natural for a group such as the JPFO to mount a damage-control effort and attempt to prevent anti-Jewish feeling from becoming even stronger among gun owners. Their strategy is to deflect the blame from their kinsmen in the media and the government and direct it onto their most hated enemies, the National Socialists—or at least to create enough smoke to obscure the facts and keep the gun-owning public confused.

Unfortunately for those who would like to link Hitler and the National Socialists with gun control, the entire premise for such an effort is false. German firearms legislation under Hitler, far from banning private ownership, actually facilitated the keeping and bearing of arms by German citizens by eliminating or ameliorating restrictive laws which had been enacted by the government preceding his: a left-center government which had contained a number of Jews.

It is not just that the National Socialist firearms legislation was the *opposite* of what it has been claimed to have been by persons who want to tar modern gun-grabbers with the "Nazi" brush: the whole spirit of Hitler's government was starkly different from its portrayal by America's mass media. The facts, in brief, are these:

- The National Socialist government of Germany, unlike the government in Washington today, did not fear its citizens. Adolf Hitler was the most popular leader Germany has ever had. Unlike American presidents, he did not have to wear body armor and have shields of bulletproof glass in front of him whenever he spoke in public. At public celebrations he rode standing in an open car as it moved slowly through cheering crowds. Communists made several attempts to assassinate him, and his government stamped down hard on communism, virtually wiping it out in Germany. Between upright, law-abiding German citizens and Adolf Hitler, however, there was a real love affair, with mutual trust and respect.
- The spirit of National Socialism was one of manliness, and individual self-defense and self-reliance were central to the National Socialist view of the way a citizen should behave. The notion of banning firearms ownership was utterly alien to National Socialism. In the German universities, where National Socialism gained its earliest footholds and which later became its strongest bastions, dueling was an accepted practice. Although the liberal-Jewish governments in Germany after the First World War attempted to ban dueling, it persisted illegally until it was again legalized by the National Socialists. Fencing, target shooting, and other martial arts were immensely popular in Germany, and the National Socialists encouraged young Germans to become proficient in

these activities, believing that they were important for the development of a man's character.

• Gun registration and licensing (for long guns as well as for handguns) were legislated by an anti-National Socialist government in Germany in 1928, *five years before the National Socialists gained power*. Hitler became Chancellor on January 30, 1933. Five years later his government got around to rewriting the gun law enacted a decade earlier by his predecessors, *substantially ameliorating* it in the process (for example, long guns were exempted from the requirement for a purchase permit; the legal age for gun ownership was lowered from 20 to 18 years; the period of validity of a permit to carry weapons was extended from one to three years; and provisions restricting the amount of ammunition or the number of firearms an individual could own were dropped). Hitler's government may be criticized for leaving certain restrictions and licensing requirements in the law, but the National Socialists had no intention of preventing law-abiding Germans from keeping or bearing arms. Again, the firearms law enacted by Hitler's government *enhanced* the rights of Germans to keep and bear arms; no new restrictions were added, and many pre-existing restrictions were relaxed or eliminated.

• At the end of the Second World War, American GIs in the occupying force were astounded to discover how many German civilians owned private firearms. Tens of thousands of pistols looted from German homes by GIs were brought back to the United States after the war. In 1945 General Eisenhower ordered all privately owned firearms in the American occupation zone of Germany confiscated, and Germans were required to hand in their shotguns and rifles as well as any handguns which had not already been stolen. In the Soviet occupation zone German civilians were summarily shot if they were found in possession of even a single cartridge.

MAUSER, Germany's foremost manufacturer of rifles and pistols, advertised its wares widely throughout the National Socialist period. This Mauser ad is for "military, hunting, sports, and self-defense weapons." It appeared in the February 1939 issue of the popular German magazine *Atlantis,* Germany's answer to the *National Geographic.*

• Jews, it should be noted, were not Germans, even if they had been born in Germany. The National Socialists defined citizenship in ethnic terms, and under Hitler Jews were not accorded full rights of citizenship. National Socialist legislation progressively excluded Jews from key professions: teaching, the media, the practice of law, etc. The aim was not only to free German life from an oppressive and degenerative Jewish influence, but to persuade Jews to emigrate. The German Weapons Law of March 18, 1938, specifically excluded Jews from manufacturing or dealing in firearms or munitions, but it did not exclude them from owning or bearing personal firearms. The exclusion of Jews from the firearms business rankled them as much as any other exclusion, and in their typically ethnocentric fashion they have misrepresented the law involved as an anti-gun law in an effort to cast their enemies in a bad light.

It should be noted in passing that the restrictions placed on Jews by the National Socialists had the intended effect: between 1933 and 1939 two-thirds of the Jews residing in Germany emigrated, reducing the Jewish population of the country from 600,000 when Hitler became Chancellor in 1933 to 200,000 at the outbreak of the Second World War in 1939. Jews in the United States, looking at this period from their own narrowly focused viewpoint, have described these peacetime years of the National Socialist government as a time of darkness, terror, and regression, whereas for the German people it was a time of hope, joy, and spiritual and material renewal.

Much the same type of distortion is seen in the portrayal of the United States in the early 1950s: the so-called "McCarthy Era." Senator Joseph McCarthy (Republican, Wisconsin) used his position as chairman of the Senate's Government Operations Committee to expose the widespread communist infiltration of the U.S. government and other U.S. institutions which had taken place during the Second World War. A substantial majority of the communists who were dragged reluctantly out into the light of day by his efforts were Jews. As a result, the controlled media always have portrayed the period as one of terror and repression, when everyone was frightened of Senator McCarthy's "witch-hunt." Of course, it was nothing of the sort to non-Jewish Americans, who were not intimidated in the least. History viewed through a Jewish lens—i.e., through media controlled by Jews—always is distorted in a way corresponding to Jewish interests and concerns.

Both the German Weapons Law of March 18, 1938, enacted by the National Socialists, and the Law on Firearms and Ammunition of April 12, 1928, which was enacted by an anti-National Socialist government, are given below in full, first in facsimile and then in English translation. A little background information first, however, may help the reader to understand their significance.

After Germany's defeat in the First World War (a defeat in which

Germany's Jews played no small part, demoralizing the home front with demonstrations and other subversive activity much as they did in America during the Vietnam war), the Kaiser abdicated, and liberals and leftists seized control of the government in 1918. Hitler, recovering in a military hospital from a British poison-gas attack which had blinded him temporarily, made the decision to go into politics and fight against the traitors he felt were responsible for Germany's distress.

The tendency of Germany's new rulers after the First World War was much the same as it is for the liberals in America today: they promoted cosmopolitanism, internationalism, and egalitarianism. By 1923 economic conditions in Germany had become catastrophic, and there was much public unrest. The communists had made major inroads into the labor movement and were a growing threat to the country.

GERMAN CIVILIANS were ordered by American occupiers to turn in all of their weapons (including fencing swords, as held by the man at the right) in 1945. They lined up at collection points all over Germany to do so. GIs were amazed that German civilians owned so many firearms. (U.S. ARMY SIGNAL CORPS PHOTO)

Hitler had indeed gone into politics, and his National Socialists battled the communists in the streets of Germany's cities and gradually came to be seen by many patriotic Germans in the working class and the middle class as the only force which could save Germany from a communist takeover and total ruin. Hitler's National Socialists continued to win recruits and gain strength during the 1920s. The communists, with aid from the Soviet Union, also continued to grow. The political situation became increasingly unstable as the government lost popular support.

The government's response was to substantially tighten up restrictions on the rights of German citizens to keep and bear arms. The Law on Firearms and Ammunition of April 12, 1928, was the most substantial effort in this regard. This law was enacted by a left-center government hostile to the National Socialists (the government was headed by Chancellor Wilhelm Marx and consisted of a coalition of Socialists, including many Jews, and Catholic Centrists).

Five years later, in 1933, the National Socialists were in power, Hitler headed the government, and the communist threat was crushed decisively. The National Socialists began undoing the social and economic damage done by their predecessors. Germany was restored to full employment, degeneracy and corruption were rooted out, Jews and their collaborators were removed from one facet of national life after another, and the German people entered a new era of national freedom, health, and prosperity.

Finally, in 1938, the National Socialist government got around to enacting a new firearms law to replace the one enacted by their opponents ten years earlier. The highlights of the 1938 law, especially as it applied to ordinary citizens rather than manufacturers or dealers, follow:

• Handguns may be purchased only on submission of a Weapons Acquisition Permit (*Waffenerwerbschein*), which must be used within one year from the date of issue. Muzzle-loading handguns are exempted from the permit requirement. [The 1928 law had required a permit for the purchase of long guns as well, but the National Socialists dropped this requirement.]

• Holders of a permit to carry weapons (*Waffenschein*) or of a hunting license do not need a Weapons Acquisition Permit in order to acquire a handgun.

• A hunting license authorizes its bearer to carry hunting weapons and handguns.

• Firearms and ammunition, as well as swords and knives, may not be sold to minors under the age of 18 years. [The age limit had been 20 years in the 1928 law.]

• Whoever carries a firearm outside of his dwelling, his place of employment, his place of business, or his fenced property must have on his person a Weapons Permit (*Waffenschein*). A permit is not required, however, for carrying a firearm for use at a police-approved shooting range.

• A permit to acquire a handgun or to carry firearms may only be issued to persons whose trustworthiness is not in question and who can show a need for a permit. In particular, a permit may not be issued to:

1. persons under the age of 18 years;

2. legally incompetent or mentally retarded persons;

3. Gypsies or vagabonds;

4. persons under mandatory police supervision [i.e., on parole] or otherwise temporarily without civil rights;

5. persons convicted of treason or high treason or known to be engaged in activities hostile to the state;

6. persons who for assault, trespass, a breach of the peace, resistance to authority, a criminal offense or misdemeanor, or a hunting or fishing violation were legally sentenced to a term of imprisonment of more than two weeks, if three years have not passed since the term of imprisonment.

• The manufacture, sale, carrying, possession, and import of the following are prohibited:

1. "trick" firearms, designed so as to conceal their function (e.g., cane guns and belt-buckle pistols);

2. any firearm equipped with a silencer and any rifle equipped with a spotlight;

3. cartridges with .22 caliber, hollow-point bullets.

That is the essence. Numerous other provisions of the law relate to firearms manufacturers, importers, and dealers; to acquisition and carrying of firearms by police, military, and other official personnel; to the maximum fees which can be charged for permits (3 *Reichsmark*); to tourists bringing firearms into Germany; and to the fines and other penalties to be levied for violations.

The requirements of "trustworthiness" and of proof of need when obtaining a permit are troubling, *but it should be noted that they were simply carried over from the 1928 law: they were not formulated by the National Socialists.* Under the National Socialists these requirements were interpreted liberally: a person who did not fall into one of the prohibited categories listed above was considered trustworthy, and a statement such as, "I often carry sums of money," was accepted as proof of need.

The prohibitions of spotlight-equipped rifles and hollow-point .22 caliber ammunition were based on considerations that the former were unsporting when used for hunting, and the latter were inhumane.

Now read the German firearms laws for yourself, either in the original German exactly as they were published by the German government in the *Reichsgesetzblatt* or in the complete English translations which are provided here. If you want to skip over most of the legal gobbledygook and go directly to the most pertinent part of the National Socialist Firearms Law—the part pertaining to the purchase, ownership, and carrying of firearms by private citizens—turn to page 35 (Part IV of the Law). Note, as already mentioned above, that two separate and distinct types of permits are referred to: a Weapons Acquisition Permit (*Waffenerwerbschein*), required only for purchasing a handgun; and a Weapons Permit (*Waffenschein*), required for carrying any firearm in public. Interestingly enough, as also mentioned above, a hunting license could take the place of both these permits.

When you have read the two laws reproduced here, you will understand that it was Hitler's enemies, not Hitler, who should be compared with the gun-control advocates in America today. Then as now it was the Jews, not the National Socialists, who wanted the people's right of self-defense restricted. You will understand that those who continue to make the claim that Hitler was a gun-grabber are either ignorant or dishonest. And you will understand that it was not until 1945, when the communist and democratic victors of the Second World War had installed occupation governments to rule over the conquered Germans that German citizens were finally and completely denied the right to armed self-defense. □

Reichsgesetzblatt

Teil I

Jahrgang 1928

Herausgegeben vom

Reichsministerium des Innern

Berlin 1928 • Verlag des Gesetzsammlungsamts

Reichsgesetzblatt

Teil I

1928	Ausgegeben zu Berlin, den 20. April 1928	Nr. 18

Gesetz über Schußwaffen und Munition. Vom 12. April 1928.

Der Reichstag hat das folgende Gesetz beschlossen, das mit Zustimmung des Reichsrats hiermit verkündet wird:

Abschnitt I

Allgemeines

§ 1

(1) Schußwaffen im Sinne dieses Gesetzes sind Waffen, bei denen ein Geschoß oder eine Schrotladung mittels Entwicklung von Explosivgasen oder Druckluft durch einen Lauf getrieben wird.

(2) Als Munition im Sinne dieses Gesetzes gilt fertige Munition zu Schußwaffen sowie Schießpulver jeder Art.

(3) Fertige oder vorgearbeitete wesentliche Teile von Schußwaffen oder Munition stehen fertigen Gegenständen dieser Art gleich.

Abschnitt II

Die Herstellung von Schußwaffen und Munition

§ 2

(1) Wer gewerbsmäßig Schußwaffen oder Munition herstellen, bearbeiten oder instandsetzen will, bedarf der Genehmigung. Als Herstellung von Munition gilt auch das Wiederladen von Patronen.

(2) Die Genehmigung oder ihre Rücknahme darf nicht von der Prüfung der Bedürfnisfrage abhängig gemacht werden.

(3) Für die Errichtung von Pulverfabriken oder sonstigen Anlagen zur Munitionsbereitung bleibt daneben die Genehmigung nach § 16 der Gewerbeordnung für das Deutsche Reich im bisherigen Umfang erforderlich.

§ 3

Die Verfügung, durch die die Genehmigung zum Gewerbebetriebe versagt oder zurückgenommen wird, kann nach den für das Rechtsmittelverfahren gegen polizeiliche Verfügungen geltenden Vorschriften der Landesgesetze angefochten werden. Wo nach diesen ein verwaltungsgerichtliches Verfahren nicht besteht oder für Fälle dieser Art nicht zulässig ist, finden die Vorschriften der §§ 20 und 21 der Gewerbeordnung für das Deutsche Reich Anwendung.

§ 4

Ist die Genehmigung endgültig versagt oder zurückgenommen worden, so kann ein neuer Antrag auf Erteilung der Genehmigung erst gestellt werden, wenn seit der Zustellung der endgültigen Entscheidung mindestens drei Jahre verflossen sind.

Abschnitt III

Der Handel mit Schußwaffen und Munition

§ 5

(1) Wer gewerbsmäßig Schußwaffen oder Munition erwerben, feilhalten oder anderen überlassen oder wer gewerbsmäßig den Erwerb oder das Überlassen solcher Waren vermitteln oder sich gewerbsmäßig zum Erwerb oder Überlassen solcher Waren erbieten will, bedarf der Genehmigung.

(2) Die Vorschriften des § 2 Abs. 2 und der §§ 3, 4 gelten entsprechend.

(Vierzehnter Tag nach Ablauf des Ausgabetags: 4. Mai 1928)

§ 6

Die Genehmigung nach § 5 darf nicht erteilt werden

1. Trödlern,
2. den im § 16 Abs. 1 Satz 2 bezeichneten Personen; Ausnahmen sind in den Grenzen des § 16 Abs. 3 zulässig.

§ 7

(1) Verboten ist der Handel mit Schußwaffen oder Munition

1. im Umherziehen,
2. auf Jahrmärkten, Schützenfesten und Messen mit Ausnahme der Mustermessen.

(2) Nicht unter das Verbot des Abs. 1 Nr. 2 fällt das Feilhalten und Überlassen der auf den Schießständen benötigten Munition.

§ 8

Öffentlichen und privaten Pfandleihen ist das Beleihen von Schußwaffen und Munition verboten.

§ 9

(1) Vom Ablauf von sechs Monaten nach Inkrafttreten dieses Gesetzes ab dürfen im Inland nur solche Schußwaffen gewerbsmäßig feilgehalten oder anderen überlassen werden, die die Firma oder das eingetragene Warenzeichen des Herstellers oder des Händlers (§ 5) und eine fortlaufende Herstellungsnummer tragen.

(2) Schußwaffen, die nicht die Firma oder das eingetragene Warenzeichen eines inländischen Herstellers tragen, müssen außer der Herstellungsnummer die Firma oder das eingetragene Warenzeichen eines im Inland wohnenden Händlers tragen.

Abschnitt IV

Erwerb, Führen, Einfuhr und Besitz von Schußwaffen und Munition

§ 10

(1) Schußwaffen oder Munition dürfen nur gegen Aushändigung eines behördlich ausgestellten Waffen- oder Munitionserwerbscheins überlassen oder erworben werden.

(2) Der Erwerbschein gilt für die Dauer eines Jahres vom Tage der Ausstellung ab gerechnet, soweit nicht eine kürzere Geltungsdauer auf ihm vermerkt ist.

(3) Abs. 1 gilt nicht für

1. die Überlassung von Schußwaffen oder Munition auf einem polizeilich genehmigten Schießstand zur Benutzung lediglich auf diesem Schießstand;
2. die Versendung von Schußwaffen oder Munition unmittelbar in das Ausland; dem Ausland im Sinne dieser Vorschrift stehen gleich:
   a) die Zollausschlüsse, mit Ausnahme von Helgoland und der Badischen Zollausschlüsse,
   b) die Freibezirke,
   c) die Freizone von Lübeck;
3. die Übermittlung von Schußwaffen und Munition durch Personen, die gewerbsmäßig Güterversendungen besorgen oder ausführen, insbesondere durch Spediteure, Frachtführer, Verfrachter eines Seeschiffes, die Post oder die Eisenbahn.

§ 11

Eines Waffen- oder Munitionserwerbscheins bedürfen nicht:

1. Behörden des Reichs oder der Länder sowie die Deutsche Reichsbahn-Gesellschaft,
2. Gemeindebehörden, denen die oberste Landesbehörde den Erwerb ohne Erwerbschein gestattet hat,
3. die im § 5 bezeichneten Gewerbetreibenden, die sich durch eine behördliche Bescheinigung ausweisen.

§ 12

Eines Waffenerwerbscheins bedürfen nicht Inhaber von Waffenscheinen in dem darin genehmigten Umfang.

§ 13

Eines Munitionserwerbscheins bedürfen nicht Inhaber eines Waffenerwerbscheins oder Waffenscheins zum Erwerbe der zu den betreffenden Waffen gehörigen Munition.

§ 14

Wer Schußwaffen oder Munition von Todes wegen erwirbt, hat dies unter Angabe der Art und Zahl, bei Schießpulver des Gewichts, der von ihm erworbenen Schußwaffen oder Munition binnen sechs Wochen nach dem Tage, an dem er von dem Erwerbe Kenntnis erlangt hat, der zuständigen Behörde anzuzeigen.

§ 15

(1) Wer außerhalb seiner Wohnung, seiner Geschäftsräume oder seines befriedeten Besitztums eine Schußwaffe führt, muß einen behördlich ausgestellten Erlaubnisschein (Waffenschein) bei sich tragen. Als Führen einer Schußwaffe gilt nicht ihr Gebrauch auf polizeilich genehmigten Schießständen.

(2) Der Waffenschein ist, sofern seine Geltung nicht ausdrücklich auf einen bestimmten engeren Bezirk beschränkt wird, für das ganze Reichsgebiet gültig. Im Scheine kann das Führen der Waffen auf bestimmte ausdrücklich bezeichnete Gelegenheiten und Örtlichkeiten beschränkt werden.

(3) Der Waffenschein gilt für die Dauer eines Jahres vom Tage der Ausstellung ab gerechnet, soweit nicht eine kürzere Geltungsdauer auf ihm vermerkt ist.

§ 16

(1) Waffen- (Munitions-) Erwerbscheine oder Waffenscheine dürfen nur an Personen, gegen deren Zuverlässigkeit keine Bedenken bestehen, ausgestellt werden, Waffenscheine außerdem nur bei Nachweis eines Bedürfnisses. Die Ausstellung hat insbesondere zu unterbleiben

1. an Personen unter zwanzig Jahren;
2. an Entmündigte oder geistig Minderwertige;

3. an Zigeuner oder nach Zigeunerart umherziehende Personen;

4. an Personen, die wegen Zuwiderhandlungen gegen die §§ 81, 83 bis 90, 105, 106, 107, 107a, 110 bis 120, 122, 123 Abs. 2, §§ 124 bis 130, 181a, 211 bis 216, 223 bis 228, 240, 241, 243, 244, 249 bis 255, 292 bis 294, 296, 340, 361 Nr. 3, 4, 5 und 10 des Strafgesetzbuchs, gegen § 148 des Vereinszollgesetzes vom 1. Juli 1869 (Bundesgesetzbl. S. 317), gegen das Gesetz gegen den verbrecherischen und gemeingefährlichen Gebrauch von Sprengstoffen vom 9. Juni 1884 (Reichsgesetzbl. S. 61), gegen die Verordnung des Rates der Volksbeauftragten über Waffenbesitz vom 13. Januar 1919 (Reichsgesetzbl. S. 31, 122), gegen das Gesetz über die Entwaffnung der Bevölkerung vom 7. August 1920 (Reichsgesetzbl. S. 1553), gegen die §§ 1, 2, 4 bis 7, 8 Nr. 3, § 19 des Gesetzes zum Schutze der Republik vom 21. Juli 1922 (Reichsgesetzbl. I S. 585) oder gegen die Vorschriften dieses Gesetzes zu einer Freiheitsstrafe von mehr als zwei Wochen rechtskräftig verurteilt worden sind, wenn seit der Verbüßung, der Verjährung oder dem Erlasse der Strafe noch nicht fünf Jahre verflossen sind; ist die Strafe nach einer Probezeit erlassen, so läuft die Frist von fünf Jahren von dem Beginne der Probezeit;

5. an Personen, gegen die auf Zulässigkeit von Polizeiaufsicht oder auf Verlust der bürgerlichen Ehrenrechte erkannt worden ist, für die Dauer der Zulässigkeit der Polizeiaufsicht oder des Verlustes der bürgerlichen Ehrenrechte.

(2) Die obersten Landesbehörden können durch Verordnung bestimmen, daß Zuwiderhandlungen gegen landesrechtliche Strafvorschriften den Zuwiderhandlungen gegen die im Abs. 1 Nr. 4 bezeichneten reichsrechtlichen Bestimmungen gleichgestellt werden.

(3) Ausnahmen von Abs. 1 Nr. 1, 3 und 4 können auf Antrag von der zuständigen Behörde bewilligt werden.

§ 17

(1) Personen, denen nach § 16 Abs. 1 Nr. 1 bis 5 ein Waffen- (Munitions-) Erwerbschein oder ein Waffenschein nicht ausgestellt werden darf, sind, wenn nicht eine Ausnahme nach § 16 Abs. 3 bewilligt ist, auch zum Besitze von Schußwaffen oder Munition nicht berechtigt.

(2) Personen, die zum Besitze von Schußwaffen oder Munition nicht berechtigt sind, haben die in ihrem Besitze befindlichen Schußwaffen und Munition unverzüglich der zuständigen Behörde gegen Empfangsbescheinigung in Verwahrung zu geben. Haben sie einen gesetzlichen Vertreter, so liegt ihm diese Verpflichtung ob. Sofern diese Person oder ihre gesetzlichen Vertreter über die Schußwaffen oder Munition nicht binnen sechs Monaten zugunsten eines im Sinne dieses Gesetzes Berechtigten durch Abtretung des Herausgabeanspruchs verfügen, kann die zuständige Behörde die Übereignung der Schußwaffen und Munition an sich gegen Zahlung des gemeinen Wertes verlangen. Der Eigentumsübergang kommt durch Zustellung des entsprechenden Bescheids zustande. Gegen die Festsetzung des gemeinen Wertes ist unter Ausschluß des Rechtswegs nur die Beschwerde im Aufsichtswege binnen zwei Wochen zulässig.

(3) Die zuständige Behörde kann ausnahmsweise dem zur Ablieferung Verpflichteten den weiteren Besitz der Schußwaffen und Munition auf jederzeitigen Widerruf gestatten, wenn nach Lage des Einzelfalls die Gewähr besteht, daß von den Gegenständen kein unzulässiger Gebrauch gemacht wird.

§ 18

(1) Der Waffen- (Munitions-) Erwerbschein oder der Waffenschein ist durch die zuständige Behörde zu widerrufen und einzuziehen, wenn die Voraussetzungen für die Erteilung des Scheines nicht gegeben waren oder nicht mehr vorliegen.

(2) Im Falle des Widerrufs kann die zuständige Behörde zugleich die Ablieferung der Schußwaffen und Munition verlangen. Die Vorschriften im § 17 Abs. 2 gelten entsprechend.

§ 19

(1) Eines Waffen- (Munitions-) Erwerbscheins oder eines Waffenscheins bedürfen hinsichtlich der ihnen dienstlich gelieferten Schußwaffen oder Munition nicht

1. die Angehörigen der deutschen Wehrmacht, die Polizeibeamten des Reichs und der Länder sowie die Grenzaufsichts- und Zollfahndungsbeamten der Reichsfinanzverwaltung;
2. Beamte oder Angestellte, denen von der zuständigen Reichs- oder Landesbehörde das Recht zum Führen von Schußwaffen bei bestimmt zu bezeichnenden dienstlichen Anlässen verliehen ist oder auf Grund gesetzlicher Vorschriften zusteht. An Stelle des Waffenscheins tritt bei ihnen eine entsprechende Bescheinigung der vorgesetzten Dienst- oder der Aufsichtsbehörde.

(2) Werden den im Abs. 1 bezeichneten Personen Schußwaffen oder Munition dienstlich nicht geliefert, oder ist das Führen anderer als der dienstlich gelieferten Schußwaffen geboten, so ist die vorgesetzte Dienst- oder die Aufsichtsbehörde befugt, ihnen eine Bescheinigung auszustellen, aus der das Recht zum Erwerbe der Schußwaffen und der Munition oder zum Führen der Schußwaffen ersichtlich ist.

§ 20

(1) Ist nach der Landesgesetzgebung die Erhebung von Gebühren für die Ausstellung des Waffenerwerbscheins oder des Waffenscheins zulässig, so bestimmt sich die Festsetzung dieser Gebühren nach den durch die Reichsregierung mit Zustimmung des Reichsrats festgesetzten Grundsätzen.

(2) Für Ausstellung eines Munitionserwerbscheins werden Gebühren nicht erhoben.

§ 21

(1) Der Jahresjagdschein eines deutschen Landes berechtigt im gesamten Reichsgebiete während der Dauer seiner Gültigkeit den Inhaber zum Erwerbe von Jagdwaffen und Faustfeuerwaffen in dem darin vermerkten Umfang und zum Erwerbe von Munition für Jagd- und Faustfeuerwaffen.

(2) Der Jagdschein eines deutschen Landes berechtigt im gesamten Reichsgebiete während der Dauer seiner Gültigkeit den Inhaber zum Führen von Jagdwaffen auf der Jagd, beim Jagdschutz und Übungsschießen sowie auf den dazu gehörigen Hin- und Rückwegen. In dem gleichen Umfang berechtigt der Jagdschein auch zum Führen einer Faustfeuerwaffe.

§ 22

(1) Die Einfuhr von Schußwaffen und Munition ist nur auf Grund eines Waffen- (Munitions-) Erwerbscheins (§ 10), eines Waffenscheins (§ 15) oder eines Jagdscheins (§ 21) in dem Umfang gestattet, in dem diese Scheine zum Erwerbe von Schußwaffen oder Munition berechtigen.

(2) Diese Vorschrift findet keine Anwendung auf die Einfuhr durch die im § 11 bezeichneten Behörden und Gewerbetreibenden.

§ 23

(1) Zum Besitz eines Waffen- oder Munitionslagers (Abs. 2), das nicht zu einem nach Maßgabe dieses Gesetzes genehmigten (§§ 2, 5) Gewerbebetriebe gehört oder sich nicht im Besitz einer der im § 11 Nr. 1 und 2 bezeichneten Behörden befindet, ist die Genehmigung der zuständigen Behörde erforderlich. Die Genehmigung darf nur Personen erteilt werden, gegen deren Zuverlässigkeit keine Bedenken bestehen. Auf die Erteilung der Genehmigung finden die Vorschriften des § 16 Abs. 1 Satz 2, Abs. 2, 3, auf ihren Widerruf die Vorschriften der §§ 17, 18 entsprechende Anwendung.

(2) Als Waffenlager gilt ein Bestand von mehr als fünf Schußwaffen der gleichen Art, als Munitionslager ein Bestand von mehr als hundert Patronen. Bei Jagdwaffen gilt als Waffenlager ein Bestand von mehr als zehn Jagdwaffen, als Munitionslager ein Bestand von mehr als tausend Jagdpatronen.

§ 24

(1) Die Herstellung, der Handel, die Einfuhr, das Führen sowie der Besitz von Schußwaffen, die zum schleunigen Zerlegen über den für Jagd- und Sportzwecke allgemein üblichen Umfang hinaus besonders eingerichtet oder in Stöcken, Schirmen, Röhren oder in ähnlicher Weise verborgen sind (sogenannte Wilddiebsgewehre), ist verboten.

(2) Verboten ist auch die Herstellung, der Handel, die Einfuhr, das Führen sowie der Besitz von Schußwaffen, die mit einer Vorrichtung zur Dämpfung des Schußknalls oder mit Gewehrscheinwerfern versehen sind. Das Verbot erstreckt sich auch auf die bezeichneten Vorrichtungen allein. Für die Herstellung solcher Waffen oder Vorrichtungen zur Ausfuhr können auf Antrag Ausnahmen bewilligt werden.

Abschnitt V

Strafbestimmungen

§ 25

(1) Mit Gefängnis bis zu drei Jahren und mit Geldstrafe oder mit einer dieser Strafen wird bestraft, wer vorsätzlich oder fahrlässig den Bestimmungen dieses Gesetzes zuwider

1. Schußwaffen, Munition oder die im § 24 Abs. 2 bezeichneten Vorrichtungen herstellt, bearbeitet, instandsetzt, beleiht, erwirbt, feilhält, anderen überläßt, den Erwerb oder das Überlassen vermittelt, sich zum Erwerb oder Überlassen erbietet, einführt oder besitzt,
2. Schußwaffen führt,
3. die ihm gemäß § 14 obliegende Anzeige nicht oder nicht rechtzeitig erstattet.

(2) Neben der Strafe können die Schußwaffen, die Munition oder die Vorrichtungen, auf die sich die strafbare Handlung bezieht, ohne Rücksicht darauf, ob sie dem Täter gehören, eingezogen werden. Ist die Verfolgung oder Verurteilung einer bestimmten Person nicht durchführbar, so kann auf die Einziehung der Schußwaffen, der Munition oder der Vorrichtungen selbständig erkannt werden.

§ 26

Wer es vorsätzlich oder fahrlässig unterläßt, zu verhindern, daß eine zu seiner Hausgemeinschaft gehörige und seiner Aufsicht oder Erziehung unterliegende Person unter zwanzig Jahren den Vorschriften dieses Gesetzes zuwider Schußwaffen, Munition oder die im § 24 Abs. 2 bezeichneten Vorrichtungen herstellt, bearbeitet, instandsetzt, beleiht, erwirbt, feilhält, anderen überläßt, den Erwerb oder das Überlassen vermittelt, sich zum Erwerb oder Überlassen erbietet, einführt, besitzt oder Schußwaffen führt, wird gemäß § 25 dieses Gesetzes bestraft.

§ 27

(1) Wer die zur Durchführung dieses Gesetzes von der Reichsregierung erlassenen Vorschriften (§ 28) vorsätzlich oder fahrlässig übertritt, wird mit Geldstrafe bis zu einhundertfünfzig Reichsmark oder mit Haft bestraft.

(2) Wer den im Abs. 1 bezeichneten Vorschriften vorsätzlich zuwiderhandelt, nachdem er wegen ihrer vorsätzlichen oder fahrlässigen Übertretung zweimal rechtskräftig verurteilt ist, wird mit Gefängnis bis zu einem Jahre und mit Geldstrafe oder mit einer dieser Strafen bestraft. Diese Vorschrift findet keine Anwendung, wenn seit der Rechtskraft der letzten Verurteilung bis zur Begehung der neuen Tat mehr als drei Jahre verflossen sind.

Abschnitt VI

Schluß- und Übergangsbestimmungen

§ 28

Die zur Durchführung dieses Gesetzes erforderlichen Vorschriften erläßt die Reichsregierung mit Zustimmung des Reichsrats. Sie kann darin insbesondere Bestimmungen über die Beaufsichtigung der Herstellung von Schußwaffen oder Munition, über den Handel mit diesen Gegenständen und über den Geschäftsbetrieb, einschließlich der Buchführung, der in den §§ 2, 5 bezeichneten Gewerbetreibenden treffen. Sie kann ferner für bestimmte Arten von Schußwaffen oder Munition Ausnahmen von den Vorschriften dieses Gesetzes zulassen.

§ 29

(1) Der Erlaß weitergehender Beschränkungen über die Herstellung, den Handel, den Erwerb, das Führen und den Besitz von Schußwaffen oder Munition durch

die Länder ist unzulässig. Dies gilt auch hinsichtlich solcher Schußwaffen und Munition, für die gemäß § 28 Satz 3 Ausnahmen von den Vorschriften dieses Gesetzes zugelassen sind.

(2) Soweit Beschränkungen der im Abs. 1 bezeichneten Art bestehen, treten sie spätestens sechs Monate nach dem Inkrafttreten dieses Gesetzes außer Kraft.

§ 30

(1) Wer beim Inkrafttreten dieses Gesetzes ein nach seinen Vorschriften (§§ 2, 5) genehmigungspflichtiges Gewerbe betreibt oder ein nach § 23 genehmigungspflichtiges Waffen- oder Munitionslager besitzt, hat die Genehmigung binnen einem Monat nach dem Inkrafttreten dieses Gesetzes zu beantragen.

(2) Die Strafbarkeit gemäß § 25 Abs. 1 Nr. 1 tritt in diesem Falle erst mit Ablauf eines Monats nach dem Inkrafttreten dieses Gesetzes oder, falls der Antrag innerhalb dieser Frist gestellt ist, mit Ablauf eines Monats nach seiner endgültigen Ablehnung ein.

§ 31

Bei Personen, die beim Inkrafttreten dieses Gesetzes Schußwaffen oder Munition besitzen, ohne nach den Vorschriften dieses Gesetzes hierzu berechtigt zu sein, tritt die Strafbarkeit gemäß § 25 Abs. 1 Nr. 1 erst mit dem Ablauf von sechs Wochen nach dem Inkrafttreten dieses Gesetzes ein.

§ 32

Auf die in den §§ 2, 5 bezeichneten Gewerbebetriebe finden die Vorschriften der Gewerbeordnung insoweit Anwendung, als nicht in diesem Gesetze besondere Bestimmungen getroffen sind.

§ 33

Unberührt bleiben die Vorschriften des Gesetzes über den Friedensschluß zwischen Deutschland und den alliierten und assoziierten Mächten vom 16. Juli 1919 (Reichsgesetzbl. S. 687) sowie die zu seiner Ausführung ergangenen gesetzlichen Bestimmungen und Anordnungen der Reichsregierung.

§ 34

(1) Dieses Gesetz tritt mit dem 1. Oktober 1928 in Kraft. Gleichzeitig wird die Verordnung des Rates der Volksbeauftragten über Waffenbesitz vom 13. Januar 1919 (Reichsgesetzbl. S. 31, 122) aufgehoben.

(2) Die auf Grund der bisherigen landesrechtlichen Vorschriften ausgestellten, zum Erwerbe von Schußwaffen oder Munition oder zum Führen von Schußwaffen berechtigenden Bescheinigungen verlieren, mit Ausnahme der Jagdscheine, spätestens sechs Monate nach dem Inkrafttreten dieses Gesetzes ihre Gültigkeit.

Berlin, den 12. April 1928.

Der Reichspräsident
von Hindenburg

Der Reichsminister des Innern
von Keudell

Verordnung über die Umrechnung ausländischer Währungen und die Befreiungsgrenze für Viehversicherungen bei Berechnung der Versicherungsteuer.

Vom 3. April 1928.

Auf Grund des § 11 Abs. 3, § 21 Abs. 2 des Versicherungsteuergesetzes in der Fassung des Artikel IX der Zweiten Steuernotverordnung vom 19. Dezember 1923 (Reichsgesetzbl. I S. 1205), des Artikel XIX § 6 der Zweiten Steuernotverordnung und des § 2 der Zweiten Verordnung zur Durchführung des Münzgesetzes vom 12. Dezember 1924 (Reichsgesetzbl. I S. 775) wird folgendes bestimmt:

§ 1

Die Verordnung über Umstellung der Versicherungsteuer auf Goldrechnung vom 28. Januar 1924 (Reichsgesetzbl. I S. 38) wird wie folgt geändert:

1. § 1 Nr. 1b Satz 2 erhält folgende Fassung:

   Der Versicherer hat die Gesamtsumme dieser Beträge nach den für die Wechselsteuer vorgeschriebenen Umrechnungssätzen in Reichsmark umzurechnen.

2. § 1 Nr. 2b erhält folgende Fassung:

   b) Ist die Versicherungssumme in ausländischer Währung bemessen, so ist sie zum Zwecke der Steuerberechnung nach den für die Wechselsteuer vorgeschriebenen Umrechnungssätzen in Reichsmark umzurechnen.

3. § 1 Nr. 3 wird gestrichen.

4. Im § 2 Abs. 1 wird hinter „§ 8 Abs. 1 Nr. 1, 4," hinzugefügt „6,".

5. Im § 2 Abs. 1 Nr. 1 wird folgende Vorschrift hinzugefügt:

   c) in Nr. 6 an die Stelle des bisherigen Naturalwerts der Betrag von 1 500 Reichsmark.

6. Die Vorschrift im vorletzten Absatz des § 2 erhält folgende Fassung:

   Sofern die Versicherungssumme, die Jahresrente oder das Krankengeld in ausländischer Währung bemessen sind, sind sie zwecks Feststellung der Befreiung nach den für die Wechselsteuer vorgeschriebenen Umrechnungssätzen in Reichsmark umzurechnen.

§ 2

Diese Verordnung ist erstmalig auf die Steueraufstellung für den Monat April 1928 anzuwenden.

Berlin, den 3. April 1928.

Der Reichsminister der Finanzen
Im Auftrag
Zarden

Law Gazette of the Reich

Part I

1928	Issued in Berlin, April 20, 1928	No. 18

[...]

Firearms and Ammunition Act

April 12, 1928

The Reichstag has passed the following Act, herewith announced with the agreement of the Reich Council:

Part I
General

§1

(1) In the context of this Act, firearms are weapons which operate on the principle of a bullet or a load of shot being forced through a barrel by means of the generation of explosive gases or compressed air.

(2) In the context of this Act, ammunition includes ready-to-use ammunition for firearms as well as gunpowder of all kinds.

(3) Finished or prefabricated essential components of firearms or ammunition are considered to be equivalent to finished objects of this kind.

Part II
Manufacture of Firearms and Ammunition

§2

(1) Anyone who manufactures, modifies or repairs firearms or ammunition on a professional basis must obtain a permit. The refilling of cartridges is considered to be equivalent to the manufacture of ammunition.

(2) The issuance as well as the revocation of a permit may not be made dependent on a determination of an applicant's need for the permit.

(3) With respect to the construction of gunpowder factories or other facilities for the manufacture of ammunition, a permit in accordance with §16 of the Trading Regulations for the German Reich remains mandatory.

§3

The order by means of which a manufacturer's permit is denied or revoked may be appealed in accordance with the regulations governing protests against police orders, as these regulations are set out in the legal codes of the German Lands. In cases where these regulations do not provide for proceedings in Administrative Court, or do not admit such proceedings in the case in question, the regulations set out in §§20 and 21 of the Trading Regulations for the German Reich apply instead.

§4

If a permit has been conclusively denied or revoked, a new application for a permit may be filed only after at least three years have passed since the conclusive decision was made known.

Part III

Dealing in Firearms and Ammunition

§5

(1) Anyone who, on a professional basis, purchases, offers for sale, or otherwise provides to others, either firearms or ammunition, or acts as mediator in the purchase or provision of such items, or offers his services to effect their purchase or provision, requires a permit to do so.

(2) The regulations of § 2 Section 2 and §§ 3, 4 apply as appropriate.

§6

A permit in accordance with § 5 may not be issued to

1. junk dealers,

2. persons specified in §16 Section 1 Clause 2; exceptions may be made in accordance with §16 Section 3.

§7

(1) Dealing in firearms is prohibited

1. to travelling vendors,

2. at festivals, events featuring shooting competitions, and fairs, with the exception of trade fairs.

(2) The selling and provision of ammunition required at shooting competitions is exempted from the regulations of Section 1 No. 2.

§8

Public and private pawn shops are not permitted to lend money on firearms and ammunition.

§9

(1) Beginning six months after this Act comes into force, only such firearms as bear the name or registered trademark of the manufacturing firm or the dealer (§5) and which bear a serial number may be professionally sold or provided to others within Germany.

(2) Firearms not identified by the name or registered trademark of a domestic manufacturer must be marked with a manufacturing number and the name or registered trademark of a domestic dealer.

Part IV

Purchase, Carrying, Importation and Ownership of Firearms and Ammunition

§10

(1) Firearms or ammunition may be provided or purchased only on submission of a Weapons or Ammunition Acquisition Permit issued by the appropriate authorities.

(2) The acquisition permit is valid for the period of one year from the date of issue, provided that a shorter period of validity has not been specified on it.

(3) Section 1 does not apply to:

1. the provision of firearms or ammunition at shooting booths or ranges licensed by the police, where the firearms and ammunition are to be used on-site only;

2. the export of firearms or ammunition directly out of the country. In the context of the present regulation, this includes the following:

a) the customs zones, with the exception of Helgoland and the customs zones of Baden,

b) the foreign trade zones,

c) the trade zone of Lübeck;

3. the conveyance of firearms and ammunition by persons who, as part of their profession, arrange for or conduct the transport of goods, particularly by haulers, carriers, ocean shipping agents, the Postal Service, or the Railway.

§11

The following do not require a Weapons or Ammunition Acquisition Permit:

1. authorities of the Reich or the Lands as well as the German Reich Railway Association;

2. community authorities whom the highest authority of their Land has granted the right of acquisition without an Acquisition Permit;

3. the professionals specified in §5 who are officially licensed.

§12

Holders of Weapons Permits do not require Weapons Acquisition Permits for weapons included in the scope of the Weapons Permits.

§13

Holders of Weapons Acquisition Permits or Weapons Permits do not require Ammunition Acquisition Permits to acquire the ammunition needed for the weapons in question.

§14

Anyone who acquires firearms or ammunition by inheritance must report this to the proper authorities within six weeks of the date of acquisition. This report must detail the kind and number of firearms and ammunition, and—in the case of gunpowder—the weight.

§15

(1) Anyone who carries a firearm outside his home, his place of business, or his fenced-in property must carry an official permit (Weapons Permit) on his person. “Carrying a firearm” does not include its use on shooting ranges officially licensed by the police.

(2) Provided that its validity is not expressly restricted to a smaller area, the Weapons Permit is valid throughout the Reich proper. Through an appropriate notation on the permit, the right to carry a firearm can be restricted to certain, clearly specified occasions and locations.

(3) A Weapons Permit is valid for a period of one year from the date of issue, provided that a shorter period is not specified.

§16

(1) Weapons (Ammunition) Acquisition Permits may only be issued to persons whose trustworthiness is not in question; further, Weapons Permits may only be issued on proven need. In particular, permits may not be issued to

1. persons under the age of 20 years;

2. legally incapacitated or mentally inferior persons;

3. Gypsies or vagabond persons;

4. persons who have been legally sentenced to a term of imprisonment of more than two weeks for violations of §§81, 83 to 90, 105, 106, 107, 107a, 110 to 120, 122, 123 Section 2, §§124 to 130, 181a, 211 to 216, 223 to 228, 240, 241, 243, 244, 249 to 255, 292 to 294, 296, 340, 361 Nos. 3, 4, 5 and 10 of the Penal Code, of §148 of the Federal Customs Regulation of July 1, 1869 (Federal Law Gazette p. 317), of the law against the criminal and dangerous use of explosives, June 9, 1884 (Law Gazette of the Reich p. 61), of the Ordinance of the Council of People's Representatives regarding the possession of weapons, January 13, 1919 (Law Gazette of the Reich p. 31, 122), of the law regarding the disarming of the people, August 7, 1920 (Law Gazette of the Reich p. 1553), of §§1, 2, 4 to 7, 8 No. 3, §19 of the Law

for the Protection of the Republic, July 21, 1922 (Law Gazette of the Reich I, p. 585), or of the stipulations of the present Act—provided that five years have not yet passed since the sentence was served, lapsed, or was remitted; if the sentence was remitted after a probationary period, the term of five years is calculated from the start of the probationary period;

5. persons under mandatory police supervision or who have been relieved of their civil rights—for as long as these remain under mandatory police supervision or remain stripped of their civil rights;

(2) The highest authorities of the Lands may decree that violations of state [Land] penal codes are to be considered equivalent to violations against the federal [Reich] laws set out in Section 1 No. 4.

(3) Exceptions to Section 1 Nos. 1, 3 and 4 may be granted on request by the relevant authorities.

§17

(1) Persons to whom a Weapons (Ammunition) Acquisition Permit or a Weapons Permit may not be issued, in accordance with §16 Section 1 Nos. 1 to 5, are also not permitted to possess firearms or ammunition, unless an exception has been granted under §16 Section 3.

(2) Persons who are not entitled to the possession of firearms or ammunition shall without delay hand in any firearms or ammunition in their possession to the appropriate authorities for safekeeping; they shall be given a written acknowledgement of receipt. If a person to whom this regulation applies has a legal representative, the responsibility to comply rests with the representative. If this person or his legal representative does not ensure that the firearms and ammunition become available to a person entitled to their possession in the spirit of the present law by relinquishing to such a person the right to claim return of the items in question, the authorities responsible can require that ownership of the firearms and ammunition be transferred to themselves [the authorities] instead, in return for the payment of their market value. Transfer of ownership is effected by means of notice being given. An appeal against the determined market value may be addressed to the supervisory authority within two weeks; recourse to legal action is not an option.

(3) The authorities responsible may, in exceptional cases, permit persons obliged by law to hand in their firearms and ammunition to retain possession of these items if the facts of the individual case guarantee that the objects will not be misused; such permission can be withdrawn at any time.

§18

(1) The Weapons (Ammunition) Acquisition Permit is to be revoked and confiscated by the authorities responsible if the prerequisites for its issue are not met, or are no longer met.

(2) In the case of revocation of a permit, the authorities responsible may demand that the firearms and ammunition be turned in at the same time. The stipulations of §17 Section 2 apply as appropriate.

§19

(1) With respect to the firearms or ammunition provided to them in the line of duty, the following persons do not require a Weapons (Ammunition) Acquisition Permit:

1. members of the German Wehrmacht, police officials in the service of the Reich or the Lands, as well as border patrol and customs investigation officials employed with the Financial Administration of the Reich;

2. government officials or employees whom the Reich or Land authorities responsible have granted the right to carry firearms at specifically defined instances in the line of duty, or to whom this right is granted by legal provisions. In such cases, the Weapons Permit is replaced by an appropriate license or certificate, issued by the superior or supervisory authority.

(2) If firearms or ammunition are not officially provided to persons specified in Section 1, or if firearms other than those officially supplied are required, the superior or supervisory

departments are authorized to issue certificates entitling these persons to purchase or carry a firearm.

§20

(1) If the legal provisions of a Land admit the levying of fees for issuing Weapons Acquisition Permits or Weapons Permits, the amount of these fees will be determined by the guidelines set jointly by the government of the Reich and the Reich Council.

(2) No fees are to be levied for issuing an Ammunition Acquisition Permit.

§21

(1) An annual hunting license issued by a German Land authorizes its owner, throughout the German Reich and for the period of the permit's validity, to acquire hunting weapons and handguns to the number indicated on the license, as well as to acquire ammunition for these hunting weapons and handguns.

(2) A hunting license issued by a German Land authorizes its owner, throughout the German Reich and for the period of the permit's validity, to carry hunting weapons on occasions of hunting, game protection and shooting practice, as well as on the return trips involved in these activities. A hunting license authorizes the carrying of a handgun in the same scope and manner.

§22

(1) Importation of firearms or ammunition is permitted only with a Weapons (Ammunition) Acquisition Permit (§10), a Weapons Permit (§15) or a hunting license (§21), and only to the extent to which these permits authorize the acquisition of firearms or ammunition.

(2) This regulation does not apply to importation by the authorities and professionals specified in §11.

§23

(1) Official authorization is required for the possession of weapons or ammunition stores (Section 2) not belonging to a professional enterprise sanctioned by this Act (§§2, 5) and not in the possession of one of the authorities set out in §11 Nos. 1 and 2. Only such persons whose trustworthiness is in no way in question may be authorized. §16 Section 1 Clause 2, Sections 2 and 3 apply as appropriate to the granting of such authorization; §§17, 18 apply as appropriate to its revocation.

(2) A weapons store is defined as a stock of more than five firearms of one and the same kind, an ammunition store as a stock of more than one hundred cartridges. For hunting weapons, a weapons store is defined as a stock of more than ten hunting weapons, an ammunition store as a stock of more than one thousand hunting cartridges.

§24

(1) Manufacturing, dealing, importation, carrying, or possession of firearms which have been specially designed to be rapidly disassembled beyond the measure usual for hunting and sports purposes, or which are concealed in canes, umbrellas, piping or in similar ways (so-called poachers' guns) is prohibited.

(2) Further, manufacturing, dealing, importation, carrying, or possession of firearms equipped with a device to silence the report of a shot, or with rifle spotlights, is prohibited. This ban also extends to these modifying devices in and of themselves. With respect to the manufacture of such weapons or devices for export purposes, exceptions may be granted upon request.

Part V
Penal Laws

§25

(1) Anyone who, in deliberate or negligent violation of the present law,

1. manufactures, modifies, repairs, lends money on, acquires, offers for sale, makes available to others, mediates in the acquisition or making available to others, imports or possesses weapons, ammunition or the devices described in §24 Section 2,

2. carries firearms, or

3. fails to file, or to file in time, the notice which it is incumbent upon him to file in accordance with §14,

will be penalized with up to three years' imprisonment and/or a monetary fine.

(2) Over and above this penalty, the weapons, ammunition or devices to which the punishable act in question relates may be confiscated regardless of whether they belong to the offender or not. If no specific individual/s can be prosecuted or convicted, confiscation of the weapons, ammunition or devices may be carried out without these concomitants.

§26

Anyone who, deliberately or through negligence, fails to prevent a person under the age of twenty years, who is a member of his household and subject to his supervision, from violating the present Act by manufacturing, modifying, repairing, lending money on, acquiring, offering for sale, making available to others, mediating in the acquisition or the making available to others, importing or possession of firearms, ammunition or the devices specified in §24 Section 2, or by carrying firearms, will be penalized in accordance with §25 of the present Act.

§27

(1) A monetary fine of up to one hundred and fifty Reichsmark or a term of imprisonment applies to anyone who deliberately or through negligence violates the juridical stipulations for the enforcement (§28) of the present Act.

(2) Anyone who deliberately violates the regulations set out in Section 1 after having been twice previously convicted for deliberate or negligent violation of the same will be penalized with a term of up to one year in prison and/or a monetary fine. This regulation does not apply if more than three years have passed since the last conviction prior to commission of the new offence.

Part VI
Final and Interim Regulations

§28

The regulations required for the enforcement of this Act will be issued by the government of the Reich, with the agreement of the Reich Council. In particular, the government of the Reich may issue regulations pertaining to the manufacture of firearms and ammunition, to dealing in such objects, and to the conduct of business, especially records-keeping, by such professionals as are set out in §§2, 5. Further, it may admit of exceptions to the regulations of the present Act which govern certain kinds of firearms or ammunition.

§29

(1) The individual Lands may not impose farther-reaching restrictions to the manufacture, dealing, acquisition, carrying and possession of firearms and ammunition. This also goes for such firearms and ammunition for which exceptions are permitted in accordance with §28 Clause 3.

(2) Any restrictions of the kind specified in Section 1 which are in effect at the present time will cease to be in force at most six months after the present law takes effect.

§30

(1) Anyone who, at the time this law takes effect, carries on business activities which require a permit in accordance with the present Act (§§2, 5), or who possesses a weapons or ammunition store requiring a permit in accordance with §23, must apply for a permit within one month from the date on which this law takes effect.

(2) A criminal offence as detailed in § 25 Section 1 No. 1 occurs if one month lapses following the coming into force of the present law, or, if a permit was applied for within this period, at the end of one month after this permit was definitely refused.

§31

In the case of persons who, at the time this law takes effect, possess firearms or ammunition without being entitled to such possession under the present law, a punishable act in accordance with §25 Section 1 No. 1 occurs six weeks after this law has taken effect.

§32

The manufacturing and trading enterprises specified in §§ 2, 5 are subject to the usual trading regulations insofar as no special regulations have been set out in the present Act.

§33

The stipulations of the law governing the peace agreement between Germany and the Allied and Associated Powers, July 16, 1919 (Law Gazette of the Reich p. 687), as well as the juridical regulations and orders issued for its implementation by the government of the Reich, remain unaffected by the present Act.

§34

(1) This law will take effect on October 1, 1928. At the same time, the Ordinance issued by the Council of People's Representatives on January 13, 1919, (Law Gazette of the Reich p. 31, 122) is repealed.

(2) With the exception of hunting licenses, the permits issued under regulations heretofore in effect and which authorize the acquisition of firearms or ammunition or the possession of firearms become invalid not later than six months after the present law takes effect.

Berlin, April 12, 1928

President of the Reich
von Hindenburg

Reich Minister of Domestic Affairs
von Keudell

Reichsgesetzblatt

Teil I

Jahrgang 1938

Herausgegeben
vom
Reichsministerium des Innern

Berlin 1938 • Reichsverlagsamt

Reichsgesetzblatt

Teil I

1938	Ausgegeben zu Berlin, den 21. März 1938	Nr. 31

Inhalt

Waffengesetz.

Vom 18. März 1938.

Die Reichsregierung hat das folgende Gesetz beschlossen, das hiermit verkündet wird:

Abschnitt I

Allgemeines

§ 1

(1) Schußwaffen im Sinne dieses Gesetzes sind Waffen, bei denen ein fester Körper durch Gas- oder Luftdruck durch einen Lauf getrieben werden kann.

(2) Als Munition im Sinne dieses Gesetzes gilt fertige Munition zu Schußwaffen sowie Schießpulver jeder Art.

(3) Fertige oder vorgearbeitete wesentliche Teile von Schußwaffen oder Munition stehen fertigen Schußwaffen oder fertiger Munition gleich.

§ 2

Hieb- oder Stoßwaffen im Sinne dieses Gesetzes sind Waffen, die ihrer Natur nach dazu bestimmt sind, durch Hieb, Stoß oder Stich Verletzungen beizubringen.

Abschnitt II

Herstellung von Schußwaffen und Munition

§ 3

(1) Wer gewerbsmäßig Schußwaffen oder Munition herstellen, bearbeiten oder instand setzen will, bedarf dazu der Erlaubnis. Als Herstellen von Munition gilt auch das Wiederladen von Patronenhülsen.

(2) Die Erlaubnis darf nur erteilt werden, wenn der Antragsteller die deutsche Staatsangehörigkeit besitzt und im Reichsgebiet einen festen Wohnsitz hat.

(3) Der Reichsminister des Innern kann im Einvernehmen mit den beteiligten Reichsministern Ausnahmen von den Vorschriften des Abs. 2 zulassen.

(4) Die Erlaubnis darf ferner nur erteilt werden, wenn der Antragsteller und die für die kaufmännische oder für die technische Leitung seines Betriebes in Aussicht genommenen Personen die für den Betrieb des Gewerbes erforderliche persönliche Zuverlässigkeit und wenn der Antragsteller oder die für die technische Leitung seines Betriebes in Aussicht genommene Person die für den Betrieb des Gewerbes erforderliche fachliche Eignung besitzen.

(5) Die Erlaubnis darf nicht erteilt werden, wenn der Antragsteller und die für die kaufmännische oder für die technische Leitung seines Betriebes in Aussicht genommenen Personen oder einer von ihnen Jude ist.

§ 4

(1) Bei der Erteilung der Erlaubnis kann eine Frist bis zur Dauer eines Jahres bestimmt werden, innerhalb deren das Gewerbe begonnen werden muß, widrigenfalls die Erlaubnis erlischt. Ist eine Frist nicht bestimmt, so erlischt die Erlaubnis, wenn das Gewerbe nicht innerhalb eines Jahres nach Erteilung der Erlaubnis begonnen wird. Die Fristen können verlängert werden, wenn ein wichtiger Grund vorliegt.

(2) Die Erlaubnis erlischt ferner, wenn der Gewerbetreibende das Gewerbe seit einem Jahr nicht mehr ausgeübt hat, ohne daß ihm darüber hinaus eine Frist gewährt worden ist, innerhalb deren das Gewerbe wieder aufgenommen werden muß. Diese Frist beträgt höchstens ein Jahr; sie kann verlängert werden, wenn ein wichtiger Grund vorliegt.

(3) Der Gewerbetreibende hat binnen einer Woche schriftlich anzuzeigen, daß er das Gewerbe begonnen hat oder nicht mehr ausübt.

§ 5

(1) Die Erlaubnis zur Ausübung des Gewerbes ist zurückzunehmen, wenn in der Person des Gewerbetreibenden oder des Leiters des Betriebes die Voraussetzungen nicht mehr vorliegen, die für die Erteilung der Erlaubnis erforderlich sind.

(2) Soll die Erlaubnis zurückgenommen werden, so kann die Weiterführung des Gewerbebetriebes mit sofortiger Wirkung vorläufig untersagt werden. Diese Maßnahme tritt außer Kraft, wenn nicht innerhalb einer Woche der Antrag auf Rücknahme der zuständigen Behörde vorgelegt wird, die über die vorläufige Untersagung vorab zu entscheiden hat; gegen diese Entscheidung ist eine Beschwerde nicht zulässig.

§ 6

Ist die Erlaubnis versagt oder zurückgenommen worden, so darf innerhalb zweier Jahre eine neue Erlaubnis nur erteilt werden, wenn besondere Umstände dies rechtfertigen.

Abschnitt III

Handel mit Waffen und Munition

§ 7

(1) Wer gewerbsmäßig Schußwaffen oder Munition erwerben, feilhalten oder anderen überlassen oder wer gewerbsmäßig den Erwerb oder das Überlassen solcher Gegenstände vermitteln oder sich gewerbsmäßig zu ihrem Erwerb oder Überlassen erbieten will, bedarf dazu der Erlaubnis.

(2) Die Vorschriften des § 3 Abs. 2 bis 5 und der §§ 4 bis 6 gelten entsprechend.

(3) Eine nach § 3 Abs. 1 erteilte Erlaubnis umfaßt zugleich die Erlaubnis, Schußwaffen und Munition gewerbsmäßig zu erwerben, feilzuhalten oder anderen zu überlassen.

§ 8

Die Erlaubnis nach § 7 darf Trödlern nicht erteilt werden.

§ 9

(1) Verboten ist der Handel mit Schußwaffen oder Munition sowie mit Hieb- oder Stoßwaffen

1. im Umherziehen,
2. auf Jahrmärkten, Schützenfesten und Messen mit Ausnahme der Mustermessen.

(2) Nicht unter das Verbot des Abs. 1 Nr. 2 fällt das Feilhalten und Überlassen der bei einem Schützenfest auf dem Schießstande benötigten Munition.

§ 10

(1) Schußwaffen, die gewerbsmäßig feilgehalten oder anderen überlassen werden, müssen die Firma des Herstellers und eine fortlaufende Herstellungsnummer tragen.

(2) Schußwaffen, die nicht die Firma eines inländischen Herstellers tragen, müssen außer den nach Abs. 1 vorgeschriebenen Angaben die Firma oder das eingetragene Warenzeichen eines im Inlande wohnenden Händlers tragen.

Abschnitt IV

Erwerb, Führen, Besitz und Einfuhr von Waffen und Munition

§ 11

(1) Faustfeuerwaffen dürfen nur gegen Aushändigung eines Waffenerwerbscheins überlassen oder erworben werden.

(2) Der Waffenerwerbschein gilt für die Dauer eines Jahres, vom Tage der Ausstellung an gerechnet.

(3) Abs. 1 gilt nicht für:

a) die Überlassung von Faustfeuerwaffen auf einem polizeilich genehmigten Schießstand zur Benutzung lediglich auf diesem Schießstand;

b) die Versendung von Faustfeuerwaffen unmittelbar in das Ausland;

c) die Übermittlung von Faustfeuerwaffen durch Personen, die gewerbsmäßig Güterversendungen besorgen oder ausführen, insbesondere durch Spediteure, Frachtführer, Verfrachter eines Seeschiffes, die Deutsche Reichspost oder die Deutsche Reichsbahn;

d) den Erwerb von Todes wegen.

§ 12

Eines Waffenerwerbscheins bedürfen nicht:

1. Behörden des Reichs oder der Länder, die Reichsbank und das Unternehmen „Reichsautobahnen";
2. Gemeinden (Gemeindeverbände), denen die oberste Landesbehörde den Erwerb ohne Erwerbschein gestattet hat;
3. die vom Stellvertreter des Führers bestimmten Dienststellen der Nationalsozialistischen Deutschen Arbeiterpartei und ihrer Gliederungen;
4. die vom Reichsminister der Luftfahrt bestimmten Dienststellen des Luftschutzes und des Nationalsozialistischen Fliegerkorps;
5. die vom Reichsminister des Innern bezeichneten Dienststellen der Technischen Nothilfe;
6. die in den §§ 3, 7 bezeichneten Gewerbetreibenden, die sich durch eine behördliche Bescheinigung ausweisen;
7. Inhaber von Waffenscheinen und Jahresjagdscheinen.

§ 13

(1) Jugendlichen unter 18 Jahren dürfen Schußwaffen und Munition sowie Hieb- oder Stoßwaffen nicht entgeltlich überlassen werden.

(2) Die zuständige Behörde kann Ausnahmen zulassen.

§ 14

(1) Wer außerhalb seines Wohn-, Dienst- oder Geschäftsraumes oder seines befriedeten Besitztums eine Schußwaffe führt, muß einen Waffenschein bei sich tragen. Als Führen einer Schußwaffe gilt nicht ihr Gebrauch auf polizeilich genehmigten Schießständen.

(2) Der Waffenschein ist, sofern seine Geltung nicht ausdrücklich auf einen bestimmten engeren Bezirk beschränkt wird, für das ganze Reichsgebiet gültig. Seine Geltung kann auf bestimmte, ausdrücklich bezeichnete Gelegenheiten oder Örtlichkeiten beschränkt werden.

(3) Der Waffenschein gilt für die Dauer von drei Jahren vom Tage der Ausstellung an gerechnet, soweit nicht eine kürzere Geltungsdauer auf ihm vermerkt ist.

§ 15

(1) Waffenerwerbscheine oder Waffenscheine dürfen nur an Personen, gegen deren Zuverlässigkeit keine Bedenken bestehen, und nur bei Nachweis eines Bedürfnisses ausgestellt werden.

(2) Die Ausstellung hat insbesondere zu unterbleiben:

1. an Personen unter 18 Jahren;
2. an Entmündigte und geistig Minderwertige;
3. an Zigeuner oder nach Zigeunerart umherziehende Personen;
4. an Personen, gegen die auf Zulässigkeit von Polizeiaufsicht oder auf Verlust der bürgerlichen Ehrenrechte erkannt worden ist, für die Dauer der Zulässigkeit der Polizeiaufsicht oder des Verlustes der bürgerlichen Ehrenrechte;
5. an Personen, die wegen Landesverrats oder Hochverrats verurteilt sind, oder gegen die Tatsachen vorliegen, die die Annahme rechtfertigen, daß sie sich staatsfeindlich betätigen;
6. an Personen, die wegen vorsätzlichen Angriffs auf das Leben oder die Gesundheit, wegen Land- oder Hausfriedensbruchs, wegen Widerstandes gegen die Staatsgewalt, wegen eines gemeingefährlichen Verbrechens oder Vergehens, wegen einer strafbaren Handlung gegen das Eigentum, wegen eines Jagdvergehens oder wegen eines Fischereivergehens zu einer Freiheitsstrafe von mehr als zwei Wochen rechtskräftig verurteilt worden sind, wenn seit Verbüßung der Strafe drei Jahre noch nicht verflossen sind. Der Verbüßung der Freiheitsstrafe steht ihre Verjährung, ihr Erlaß oder ihre Umwandlung in eine Geldstrafe gleich; in diesem Falle beginnt die dreijährige Frist mit dem Tage, an dem die Freiheitsstrafe verjährt oder erlassen oder in eine Geldstrafe umgewandelt worden ist. Ist die Strafe nach einer Probezeit ganz oder teilweise erlassen, so wird die Probezeit auf die Frist angerechnet.

(3) Ausnahmen von Abs. 2 Nrn. 1 und 6 können auf Antrag bewilligt werden.

§ 16

Für die Ausstellung eines Waffenerwerbscheins oder eines Waffenscheins werden nach näherer Bestimmung in der Durchführungsverordnung Gebühren erhoben.

§ 17

Der Waffenerwerbschein oder der Waffenschein ist zu widerrufen und einzuziehen, wenn die Voraussetzungen für die Erteilung des Scheines nicht gegeben waren oder nicht mehr vorliegen.

§ 18

Eines Waffenerwerbscheins oder eines Waffenscheins bedürfen hinsichtlich der ihnen dienstlich gelieferten Schußwaffen nicht:

1. die Angehörigen der Wehrmacht;
2. die Polizeibeamten einschließlich der Bahnpolizeibeamten, die Bahnschutzangehörigen im Bahnschutzdienst und die Postschutzangehörigen im Postschutzdienst;
3. die Angehörigen der SS-Verfügungstruppe und der SS-Totenkopfverbände;
4. die Beamten der Vollzugsanstalten der Reichsjustizverwaltung;
5. die im Grenzaufsichts-, Grenzabfertigungs- und Zollfahndungsdienst verwendeten Amtsträger der Reichsfinanzverwaltung;
6. die Bediensteten des Unternehmens „Reichsautobahnen", zu deren Aufgabenkreis die Überwachung der Kraftfahrbahnen gehört;
7. die im Forst-, Feld- und Jagdschutz verwendeten Beamten und Angestellten, die entweder einen Diensteid geleistet haben oder auf Grund der gesetzlichen Vorschriften als Forst-, Feld- oder Jagdschutzberechtigte eidlich verpflichtet oder amtlich bestätigt sind, sowie die Fischereibeamten und die amtlich verpflichteten Fischereiaufseher.

§ 19

(1) Eines Waffenerwerbscheins oder eines Waffenscheins bedürfen hinsichtlich der ihnen dienstlich gelieferten Schußwaffen ferner nicht:

1. im Dienste des Reichs, der Länder, der Reichsbank oder des Unternehmens „Reichsautobahnen" verwendete Personen, denen von der zuständigen Reichs- oder Landesbehörde, der Reichsbank oder dem Unternehmen „Reichsautobahnen" das Recht zum Führen von Schußwaffen verliehen ist;
2. Unterführer der Nationalsozialistischen Deutschen Arbeiterpartei vom Ortsgruppenleiter aufwärts, der SA, der SS und des Nationalsozialistischen Kraftfahrkorps vom Sturmführer aufwärts sowie der Hitlerjugend vom Bannführer aufwärts, denen von dem Stellvertreter des Führers oder der von diesem bestimmten Stelle das Recht zum Führen von Schußwaffen verliehen ist; ferner die Angehörigen der SA-Wachstandarte Feldherrnhalle in den Fällen, in denen es der Führer bestimmt;
3. Führer der Technischen Nothilfe, denen vom Reichsminister des Innern das Recht zum Führen von Schußwaffen verliehen ist;
4. Personen im Luftschutzdienst, denen vom Reichsminister der Luftfahrt oder der von diesem bestimmten Stelle das Recht zum Führen von Schußwaffen verliehen ist; der Reichsminister der Luftfahrt bestimmt im Einvernehmen mit dem Reichsminister des Innern, welche Gruppen von Personen hierfür in Frage kommen;
5. Führer im Nationalsozialistischen Fliegerkorps vom Sturmführer und selbständigen Truppführer aufwärts und selbständige Leiter von

Schulen, denen vom Reichsminister der Luftfahrt oder der von diesem bestimmten Stelle das Recht zum Führen von Schußwaffen verliehen ist.

(2) An die Stelle des Waffenscheins tritt bei ihnen eine entsprechende Bescheinigung, die für die im Abs. 1 Nrn. 1, 3 bis 5 bezeichneten Personen von der vorgesetzten Dienst- oder der Aufsichtsstelle, für die im Abs. 1 Nr. 2 bezeichneten Personen von dem Stellvertreter des Führers oder der von diesem bestimmten Stelle ausgestellt wird.

§ 20

Werden den in den §§ 18, 19 bezeichneten Personen Schußwaffen dienstlich nicht geliefert oder ist das Führen anderer als der dienstlich gelieferten Waffen geboten, so ist die vorgesetzte Dienst- oder die Aufsichtsstelle, bei den im § 19 Abs. 1 Nr. 2 bezeichneten Personen der Stellvertreter des Führers oder die von diesem bestimmte Stelle befugt, ihnen eine Bescheinigung auszustellen, aus der das Recht zum Erwerb oder zum Führen einer Schußwaffe ersichtlich ist.

§ 21

Der Jagdschein berechtigt den Inhaber zum Führen von Jagd- und Faustfeuerwaffen.

§ 22

(1) Der Erwerb von Kriegsgerät ist nur mit Erlaubnis des Oberkommandos der Wehrmacht oder der von ihm bestimmten Stellen zulässig.

(2) Der Begriff des Kriegsgeräts bestimmt sich nach den Vorschriften des Gesetzes über Aus- und Einfuhr von Kriegsgerät vom 6. November 1935 (Reichsgesetzbl. I S. 1337).

§ 23

(1) Im Einzelfalle kann einer Person, die sich staatsfeindlich betätigt hat oder durch die eine Gefährdung der öffentlichen Sicherheit zu befürchten ist, Erwerb, Besitz und Führen von Schußwaffen und Munition sowie von Hieb- oder Stoßwaffen verboten werden.

(2) Waffen und Munition, die sich im Besitz der Person befinden, gegen die das Verbot ausgesprochen ist, sind entschädigungslos einzuziehen.

§ 24

(1) Die Einfuhr von Schußwaffen und Munition über die Zollgrenze bedarf der Erlaubnis. Die Erlaubnis ist zu versagen, wenn gegen die Zuverlässigkeit des Einführenden Bedenken bestehen. Für die Erteilung und den Widerruf der Erlaubnis gelten sinngemäß die Vorschriften des § 15 Abs. 2, 3 und des § 17.

(2) Abs. 1 findet keine Anwendung auf die Einfuhr durch Behörden des Reichs oder der Länder sowie durch die in den §§ 3, 7 bezeichneten Gewerbetreibenden, die sich durch eine behördliche Bescheinigung ausweisen.

(3) Die Vorschriften des Gesetzes über Aus- und Einfuhr von Kriegsgerät vom 6. November 1935 (Reichsgesetzbl. I S. 1337) bleiben unberührt.

(4) In den Zollausschlüssen und Freibezirken werden Schußwaffen und Munition nach Maßgabe der vom Reichsminister der Finanzen im Einvernehmen mit dem Reichsminister des Innern zu erlassenden Vorschriften überwacht.

§ 25

(1) Verboten sind Herstellung, Handel, Führen, Besitz und Einfuhr

1. von Schußwaffen, die zum Zusammenklappen, Zusammenschieben, Verkürzen oder zum schleunigen Zerlegen über den für Jagd- und Sportzwecke allgemein üblichen Umfang hinaus besonders eingerichtet oder die in Stöcken, Schirmen, Röhren oder in ähnlicher Weise verborgen sind;
2. von Schußwaffen, die mit einer Vorrichtung zur Dämpfung des Schußknalles oder mit Gewehrscheinwerfern versehen sind; das Verbot erstreckt sich auch auf die bezeichneten Vorrichtungen allein;
3. von Patronen Kaliber .22 (= 5,6 mm) kurz, lang oder lang für Büchsen (Kleinkaliberpatronen) mit Hohlspitzgeschoß (Loch- oder Kerbgeschoß).

(2) Für die Ausfuhr können Herstellung, Handel und Besitz der im Abs. 1 bezeichneten Schußwaffen, Vorrichtungen und Patronen gestattet werden.

Abschnitt V

Strafbestimmungen

§ 26

(1) Mit Gefängnis bis zu drei Jahren und mit Geldstrafe oder mit einer dieser Strafen wird bestraft, wer vorsätzlich oder fahrlässig den Bestimmungen dieses Gesetzes zuwider

1. Waffen, Munition oder die im § 25 Abs. 1 Nr. 2 bezeichneten Vorrichtungen herstellt, bearbeitet, instand setzt, erwirbt, feilhält, anderen überläßt, besitzt oder einführt, den Erwerb oder das Überlassen solcher Gegenstände vermittelt oder sich zu ihrem Erwerb oder Überlassen erbietet,
2. Schußwaffen führt.

(2) Neben der Strafe können die Waffen, die Munition oder die Vorrichtungen, auf die sich die strafbare Handlung bezieht, ohne Rücksicht darauf, ob sie dem Täter gehören, eingezogen werden. Kann keine bestimmte Person verfolgt oder verurteilt werden, so kann auf die Einziehung selbständig erkannt werden, wenn im übrigen die Voraussetzungen hierfür vorliegen.

§ 27

(1) Mit Geldstrafe bis zu einhundertfünfzig Reichsmark oder mit Haft wird bestraft,

1. wer die nach § 4 Abs. 3 erforderliche Anzeige vorsätzlich oder fahrlässig nicht oder nicht rechtzeitig erstattet,
2. wer den zur Durchführung oder Ergänzung dieses Gesetzes erlassenen Rechtsvorschriften (§ 24 Abs. 4, § 31) vorsätzlich oder fahrlässig zuwiderhandelt.

(2) Wer den im Abs. 1 Nr. 2 bezeichneten Vorschriften vorsätzlich zuwiderhandelt, nachdem er wegen ihrer vorsätzlichen oder fahrlässigen Übertretung zweimal rechtskräftig verurteilt ist, wird mit Gefängnis bis zu einem Jahre und mit Geldstrafe oder mit einer dieser Strafen bestraft. Diese Vorschrift findet keine Anwendung, wenn seit der Rechtskraft der letzten Verurteilung bis zur Begehung der neuen Tat mehr als drei Jahre verflossen sind.

Abschnitt VI

Schluß- und Übergangsbestimmungen

§ 28

Auf die in den §§ 3, 7 bezeichneten Gewerbebetriebe finden die Vorschriften der Gewerbeordnung insoweit Anwendung, als nicht in diesem Gesetz besondere Bestimmungen getroffen sind.

§ 29

(1) Wer beim Inkrafttreten dieses Gesetzes zum Betrieb eines der in den §§ 3, 7 bezeichneten Gewerbebetriebe berechtigt ist, bedarf keiner neuen Erlaubnis auf Grund dieses Gesetzes. Die nach den Vorschriften des Gesetzes über Schußwaffen und Munition vom 12. April 1928 (Reichsgesetzbl. I S. 143) erteilte Genehmigung ist jedoch bis zum 31. März 1939 zu widerrufen, wenn zu diesem Zeitpunkt die im § 3 Abs. 2 bis 5 bestimmten Voraussetzungen nicht vorliegen. Für Waffenhersteller bedarf es dabei eines Nachweises der fachlichen Eignung dann nicht, wenn sie beim Inkrafttreten dieses Gesetzes ihr Gewerbe ununterbrochen mindestens fünf Jahre lang ausgeübt haben. Die auf Grund des § 5 des Gesetzes über Schußwaffen und Munition erteilte Genehmigung zum Handel mit Schußwaffen oder Munition kann bis zum 31. März 1939 ferner widerrufen werden, wenn ein Bedürfnis für die Aufrechterhaltung dieser Genehmigung örtlich nicht besteht.

(2) Bedurfte der Gewerbetreibende bisher keiner Genehmigung, weil es sich um Schußwaffen oder um Munition handelte, die den Vorschriften des Gesetzes über Schußwaffen und Munition vom 12. April 1928 (Reichsgesetzbl. I S. 143) nicht unterlagen, so ist, wenn die Schußwaffen oder die Munition den Vorschriften dieses Gesetzes unterliegen, die Erlaubnis nach §§ 3, 7 binnen eines Monats nach dem Inkrafttreten dieses Gesetzes zu beantragen.

(3) Im Falle des Abs. 2 tritt die Strafbarkeit nach § 26 Abs. 1 Nr. 1 erst mit dem Ablauf eines Monats nach dem Inkrafttreten dieses Gesetzes oder, falls der Antrag innerhalb dieser Frist gestellt ist, mit Ablauf eines Monats nach seiner endgültigen Ablehnung ein.

§ 30

(1) Schußwaffen, die nicht die im § 10 vorgeschriebene Kennzeichnung tragen, dürfen noch bis zum Ablauf eines Jahres nach dem Inkrafttreten dieses Gesetzes gewerbsmäßig feilgehalten oder anderen überlassen werden, wenn ihre Kennzeichnung den Vorschriften des § 9 des Gesetzes über Schußwaffen und Munition vom 12. April 1928 (Reichsgesetzbl. I S. 143) entspricht oder wenn sie diesen Vorschriften nicht unterlagen.

(2) Bei Schußwaffen, die nicht den Vorschriften des § 9 des Gesetzes über Schußwaffen und Munition vom 12. April 1928 (Reichsgesetzbl. I S. 143) unterlagen und bei denen die Firma des Herstellers nicht mehr festzustellen ist, erloschen ist oder bis zum Ablauf eines Jahres nach dem Inkrafttreten dieses Gesetzes erlischt, genügt statt der im § 10 dieses Gesetzes vorgeschriebenen Kennzeichnung die Angabe der Firma oder des eingetragenen Warenzeichens eines im Inlande wohnenden Händlers auf der Schußwaffe.

§ 31

Der Reichsminister des Innern erläßt die zur Durchführung und Ergänzung dieses Gesetzes erforderlichen Rechts- und Verwaltungsvorschriften. Er kann für bestimmte Arten von Waffen oder Munition Ausnahmen von den Vorschriften dieses Gesetzes zulassen.

§ 32

Weitergehende landesrechtliche Beschränkungen der Herstellung, des Handels, des Erwerbs, des Führens oder des Besitzes von Hieb- oder Stoßwaffen, mit Ausnahme der für Zigeuner oder nach Zigeunerart umherziehende Personen geltenden Vorschriften, treten spätestens sechs Monate nach Inkrafttreten dieses Gesetzes außer Kraft.

§ 33

(1) Dieses Gesetz tritt am 1. April 1938 in Kraft.

(2) Gleichzeitig treten außer Kraft:

1. das Gesetz über Schußwaffen und Munition vom 12. April 1928 (Reichsgesetzbl. I S. 143);
2. die Ausführungsverordnung zu dem Gesetz über Schußwaffen und Munition vom 13. Juli 1928 (Reichsgesetzbl. I S. 198) in der Fassung der Verordnung vom 2. Juni 1932 (Reichsgesetzbl. I S. 253);
3. das Gesetz gegen Waffenmißbrauch vom 28. März 1931 (Reichsgesetzbl. I S. 77) in der Fassung des § 10 der Verordnung des Reichspräsidenten zur Erhaltung des inneren Friedens vom 19. Dezember 1932 (Reichsgesetzbl. I S. 548);
4. Kapitel I (Maßnahmen gegen Waffenmißbrauch) des 8. Teils der Vierten Verordnung des Reichspräsidenten zur Sicherung von Wirtschaft und Finanzen und zum Schutze des inneren Friedens vom 8. Dezember 1931 (Reichsgesetzbl. I S. 699, 742);
5. § 56 Abs. 2 Ziffer 8 der Gewerbeordnung.

(3) Die Inkraftsetzung dieses Gesetzes für das Land Österreich bleibt vorbehalten.

Berlin, den 18. März 1938.

Der Führer und Reichskanzler
Adolf Hitler

Der Reichsminister des Innern
Frick

Verordnung zur Durchführung des Waffengesetzes.

Vom 19. März 1938.

Auf Grund des § 31 des Waffengesetzes vom 18. März 1938 (Reichsgesetzbl. I S. 265) wird folgendes verordnet:

Abschnitt I

Allgemeines

§ 1

(1) Höhere Verwaltungsbehörde im Sinne dieser Verordnung ist in Preußen und Bayern der Regierungspräsident (in Berlin der Polizeipräsident), in Sachsen der Kreishauptmann, im Saarland der Reichskommissar für das Saarland und im übrigen die oberste Landesbehörde.

(2) Kreispolizeibehörde im Sinne dieser Verordnung ist in Gemeinden mit staatlicher Polizeiverwaltung die staatliche Polizeibehörde, im übrigen

in Stadtkreisen ...... der Oberbürgermeister,

in Landkreisen ...... in Preußen der Landrat, in den anderen Ländern die ihm entsprechende Behörde.

§ 2

(1) Gegen Verfügungen der Verwaltungsbehörden auf Grund des Waffengesetzes und dieser Verordnung ist binnen zwei Wochen ausschließlich die Beschwerde an die vorgesetzte Verwaltungsbehörde zulässig. Diese entscheidet endgültig.

(2) Gegen Verfügungen des Polizeipräsidenten in Berlin als Orts- oder Kreispolizeibehörde ist statt der Beschwerde der Einspruch zulässig. Die Entscheidung über den Einspruch ist dem Polizeipräsidenten selbst, seinem allgemeinen Vertreter oder einem Abteilungsleiter des Polizeipräsidiums in Berlin vorbehalten.

§ 3

(1) Als wesentliche Teile im Sinne des § 1 Abs. 3 des Gesetzes sind anzusehen

a) bei Schußwaffen: Lauf, Verschluß, Trommel;

b) bei Munition: Hülse, Geschoß.

(2) Als vorgearbeitete wesentliche Teile im Sinne des § 1 Abs. 3 des Gesetzes sind nur solche im Abs. 1 bezeichneten Gegenstände anzusehen, die sich in einem derart vorgeschrittenen Herstellungszustande befinden, daß sie ohne besondere maschinelle Vorrichtungen fertig gearbeitet und zur Zusammensetzung gebrauchsfähiger Schußwaffen oder gebrauchsfähiger Munition verwendet werden können.

§ 4

Druckluftwaffen mit einem Kaliber von 7 mm und darunter unterliegen den Vorschriften des Gesetzes mit Ausnahme der §§ 9, 24 und 25 nicht.

Abschnitt II

Herstellung von Schußwaffen und Munition und Handel mit diesen Gegenständen

§ 5

Zur Erteilung und Rücknahme der Herstellungserlaubnis (§ 3 des Gesetzes) ist die höhere Verwaltungsbehörde zuständig, in deren Bezirk der Gewerbetreibende seine gewerbliche Niederlassung hat oder begründen will.

§ 6

Zur Erteilung und Rücknahme der Handelserlaubnis (§ 7 des Gesetzes) ist die Kreispolizeibehörde zuständig, in deren Bezirk der Handeltreibende seine gewerbliche Niederlassung hat oder begründen will.

§ 7

Die Herstellungs- und die Handelserlaubnis kann auf bestimmte Arten von Schußwaffen und Munition beschränkt werden.

§ 8

(1) Ob die für den Betrieb des Herstellungs- oder Handelsgewerbes erforderliche persönliche Zuverlässigkeit vorliegt (§ 3 Abs. 4, § 7 Abs. 2 des Gesetzes) ist unter Berücksichtigung des gesamten Vorlebens des Antragstellers und der Betriebsleiter zu prüfen.

(2) Die persönliche Zuverlässigkeit besitzen insbesondere nicht Personen,

1. die geschäftsunfähig oder in der Geschäftsfähigkeit beschränkt sind;
2. gegen die auf Zulässigkeit von Polizeiaufsicht oder auf Verlust der bürgerlichen Ehrenrechte erkannt worden ist, für die Dauer der Zulässigkeit der Polizeiaufsicht oder des Verlustes der bürgerlichen Ehrenrechte;
3. die wegen Landesverrats oder Hochverrats verurteilt sind oder gegen die Tatsachen vorliegen, die die Annahme rechtfertigen, daß sie sich staatsfeindlich betätigen;

4. die wegen vorsätzlichen Angriffs auf das Leben oder die Gesundheit, wegen Land- oder Hausfriedensbruchs, wegen Widerstandes gegen die Staatsgewalt, wegen eines gemeingefährlichen Verbrechens oder Vergehens, wegen einer strafbaren Handlung aus Gewinnsucht oder gegen das Eigentum oder wegen Jagdvergehens zu einer Freiheitsstrafe von mindestens drei Monaten verurteilt sind, wenn seit Verbüßung der Strafe drei Jahre noch nicht verflossen sind. Der Verbüßung der Freiheitsstrafe steht ihre Verjährung, ihr Erlaß oder ihre Umwandlung in eine Geldstrafe gleich; in diesem Falle beginnt die dreijährige Frist mit dem Tage, an dem die Freiheitsstrafe verjährt oder erlassen oder in eine Geldstrafe umgewandelt worden ist. Ist die Strafe nach einer Probezeit ganz oder teilweise erlassen, so wird die Probezeit auf die Frist angerechnet.

§ 9

(1) Die fachliche Eignung für das Herstellungsgewerbe (§ 3 Abs. 4 des Gesetzes) besitzt nur, wer entweder die Meisterprüfung für das von ihm betriebene oder für ein diesem verwandtes Handwerk bestanden hat, oder wer die Befugnis zur Anleitung von Lehrlingen in einem dieser Handwerke besitzt. Der Meisterprüfung stehen die gemäß § 133 Abs. 10 der Gewerbeordnung anerkannten Prüfungen gleich. Der Deutsche Handwerks- und Gewerbekammertag bestimmt, welche Handwerke als verwandt im Sinne dieser Verordnung gelten.

(2) Die fachliche Eignung für das Herstellungsgewerbe besitzt ferner, wer seine Sachkunde durch den erfolgreichen Besuch einer Hochschule oder einer staatlich anerkannten Fachschule oder vor einer von der Industrie- und Handelskammer zu bestimmenden Stelle nachweist. Die näheren Bestimmungen über die fachlichen Anforderungen und das Prüfungsverfahren erläßt der Reichswirtschaftsminister im Einvernehmen mit dem Reichsminister des Innern.

§ 10

Juristischen Personen des Auslands und juristischen Personen, deren Kapital sich überwiegend in ausländischen Händen befindet, darf die Erlaubnis zum Betriebe des Herstellungs- oder Handelsgewerbes nicht erteilt werden.

§ 11

Die fachliche Eignung für das Handelsgewerbe (§ 7 Abs. 2 des Gesetzes) besitzt nur, wer entweder mindestens drei Jahre Inhaber eines Geschäfts gewesen ist, in dem Schußwaffen oder Munition verkauft worden sind, oder wer in einem solchen Geschäft mindestens drei Jahre als Verkäufer, Gehilfe oder Lehrling tätig gewesen ist, oder wer seine Sachkunde vor einer von der Industrie- und Handelskammer zu bestimmenden Stelle nachweist. Die näheren Bestimmungen über die fachlichen Anforderungen und das Prüfungsverfahren erläßt der Reichswirtschaftsminister im Einvernehmen mit dem Reichsminister des Innern.

§ 12

Den Beginn oder die Einstellung des Gewerbes (§ 4 Abs. 3 des Gesetzes) hat ein Herstellungsbetrieb der höheren Verwaltungsbehörde, ein Handelsbetrieb der Kreispolizeibehörde des Bezirks anzuzeigen, in dem der Gewerbetreibende seine gewerbliche Niederlassung hat.

§ 13

Die Erlaubnis zum Betriebe des Herstellungs- oder Handelsgewerbes ist stets dann zurückzunehmen (§§ 5, 7 Abs. 2 des Gesetzes), wenn bei Erteilung der Erlaubnis der zuständigen Behörde nicht bekannt war, daß einer der im § 3 Abs. 2 bis 5 des Gesetzes oder im § 8 Abs. 2 dieser Verordnung bezeichneten Versagungsgründe vorlag oder wenn nachträglich einer dieser Fälle eintritt. Wegen Verlustes oder Beschränkung der Geschäftsfähigkeit (§ 8 Abs. 2 Nr. 1 dieser Verordnung) ist die Erlaubnis nur zurückzunehmen, wenn kein Stellvertreter gemäß § 45 der Gewerbeordnung bestellt wird.

§ 14

Zur vorläufigen Untersagung der Weiterführung des Gewerbebetriebes (§ 5 Abs. 2 des Gesetzes) ist bei einem Herstellungsgewerbe die Kreispolizeibehörde, bei einem Handelsgewerbe die Ortspolizeibehörde zuständig, in deren Bezirk der Gewerbetreibende seine gewerbliche Niederlassung hat.

§ 15

(1) Wer gewerbsmäßig Schußwaffen herstellt, hat ein Waffenbuch zu führen, aus dem der Verbleib der Schußwaffen hervorgeht. Das Waffenbuch ist nach folgendem Muster anzulegen:

Lfde. Nr.	Datum	Zahl	Art	Aufgedruckte Firma	Herstellungsnummer	Name, Wohnort und Wohnung des Erwerbers
1	2	3	4	5	6	7

(2) Kriegsgerät wird in ein besonderes Waffenbuch eingetragen.

§ 16

(1) Wer gewerbsmäßig Faustfeuerwaffen erwirbt, feilhält oder anderen überläßt oder sich gewerbsmäßig zum Erwerb oder Überlassen solcher Gegenstände er-

bietet, hat ein Waffenhandelsbuch zu führen, aus dem die Herkunft und der Verbleib der Faustfeuerwaffen hervorgehen. Das Waffenhandelsbuch ist nach folgendem Muster anzulegen:

(Linke Seite)

Einnahme

Lfde. Nr.	Datum	Zahl	Art	Aufgedruckte Firma oder Warenzeichen	Herstellungsnummer	Name und Wohnort des Überlassers
1	2	3	4	5	6	7

(Rechte Seite)

Ausgabe

Lfde. Nr.	Datum	Zahl	Art	Aufgedruckte Firma oder Warenzeichen	Herstellungsnummer	Name, Wohnort und Wohnung des Erwerbers	Nachweis der Erwerbsberechtigung
8	9	10	11	12	13	14	15

(2) Der Veräußerer hat sich davon zu überzeugen, daß der Erwerber zum Erwerb von Faustfeuerwaffen berechtigt ist. Zu diesem Zweck hat er sich den Waffenerwerbschein, Waffenschein oder Jahresjagdschein vorlegen zu lassen und in Spalte 15 des Waffenhandelsbuchs Art, Datum und Nummer des Scheines sowie die Behörde, die den Schein ausgestellt hat, zu vermerken. Ist der Erwerber zum Erwerb von Faustfeuerwaffen ohne Waffenerwerbschein, Waffenschein oder Jahresjagdschein berechtigt, so ist dies in Spalte 15 zu vermerken (z. B. Reichsbehörde, Waffenhändler).

§ 17

Für das gewerbsmäßige Vermitteln des Erwerbes oder des Überlassens von Faustfeuerwaffen ist das Waffenhandelsbuch (§ 16) nach folgendem Muster anzulegen:

Lfde. Nr.	Datum	Zahl	Art	Name, Wohnort und Wohnung des Überlassers	des Erwerbers
1	2	3	4	5	6

§ 18

(1) Das Waffen- und Waffenhandelsbuch (§§ 15 bis 17) muß dauerhaft gebunden und mit fortlaufenden Seitenzahlen versehen sein. Bevor es in Gebrauch genommen wird, ist es von der Ortspolizeibehörde unter Beglaubigung der Seitenzahl abzustempeln. In dem Buche dürfen weder Rasuren vorgenommen noch Eintragungen unleserlich gemacht werden. Alle Eintragungen müssen in deutscher Sprache und mit Tinte oder Tintenstift bewirkt werden. Das Buch ist zum 31. Dezember eines jeden Jahres sowie beim Wechsel oder bei der Einstellung des Betriebes unter Hinzufügung von Datum und Namensunterschrift so abzuschließen, daß nachträglich Eintragungen nicht mehr vorgenommen werden können. Binnen eines Monats nach Beginn des nächsten Kalenderjahres oder nach dem Wechsel des Betriebes ist das Buch der Ortspolizeibehörde zur Bestätigung des Abschlusses einzureichen. Der beim Abschluß des Buches verbliebene Bestand ist vorzutragen, bevor neue Eintragungen vorgenommen werden. Das Buch ist stets auf dem laufenden zu halten und mit den erforderlichen Unterlagen der Polizeibehörde oder deren Beauftragten auf Verlangen vorzulegen.

(2) Der Gewerbetreibende ist verpflichtet, das Buch bis zum Ablauf von zehn Jahren, von dem Tage der darin vorgenommenen letzten Eintragung an gerechnet, aufzubewahren. Gibt der Gewerbetreibende das Gewerbe auf, so hat er die von ihm geführten Bücher der Ortspolizeibehörde zur Aufbewahrung zu übergeben.

(3) Die Vorschriften der Abs. 1 und 2 gelten auch für das Waffenbuch für Kriegsgerät mit der Maßgabe, daß an die Stelle der Ortspolizeibehörde eine vom Oberkommando der Wehrmacht zu bestimmende Dienststelle der Wehrmacht tritt.

§ 19

(1) Als Hersteller im Sinne des § 10 des Gesetzes gilt auch, wer in seinem Betriebe gewerbsmäßig Schußwaffen aus Teilen, die in anderen inländischen Betrieben gefertigt sind, zusammensetzt.

(2) Werden Schußwaffen im Inland aus Teilen, die in ausländischen Betrieben gefertigt sind, zusammengesetzt, so müssen sie die Firma und die Herstellungsnummer desjenigen ausländischen Herstellers tragen, der den Lauf hergestellt hat.

(3) Den Vorschriften des § 10 des Gesetzes unterliegen nicht:

1. Vorderladerwaffen;
2. Gewehrmodelle bis zum Konstruktionsjahr 1870 einschließlich;
3. Schreckschußwaffen (Waffen, aus denen nur Knallpatronen verfeuert werden können);
4. Gas-, Betäubungs- und Scheintodwaffen (Waffen, die für Gas-, Betäubungs- oder Scheintod-

patronen bestimmt sind) mit einem Kaliber von 12 mm und darunter, wenn bei ihnen durch besondere Vorrichtungen das wirksame Verfeuern einer Kugel- oder Schrotpatrone unmöglich gemacht ist;

5. Selbstschußapparate;
6. Viehbetäubungsapparate.

Abschnitt III

Erwerb, Führen, Besitz und Einfuhr von Waffen und Munition

§ 20

Eines Waffenerwerbscheins bedarf es nicht zum Überlassen oder Erwerbe folgender Faustfeuerwaffen:

1. Vorderladerpistolen oder -revolver;
2. Schreckschußwaffen (Waffen, aus denen nur Knallpatronen verfeuert werden können);
3. Gas-, Betäubungs- und Scheintodwaffen (Waffen, die für Gas-, Betäubungs- oder Scheintodpatronen bestimmt sind) mit einem Kaliber von 12 mm und darunter, wenn bei ihnen durch besondere Vorrichtungen das wirksame Verfeuern einer Kugel- oder Schrotpatrone unmöglich gemacht ist.

§ 21

Nach § 11 Abs. 3 Buchstabe b des Gesetzes bedarf es nicht der Aushändigung eines Waffenerwerbscheins zur Versendung von Faustfeuerwaffen unmittelbar in das Ausland. Dem Ausland im Sinne dieser Vorschrift stehen gleich

1. die Zollausschlüsse, mit Ausnahme von Helgoland und der Badischen Zollausschlüsse,
2. die Freibezirke und Freizonen.

§ 22

(1) Eines Waffenscheins bedarf es nicht zum Führen folgender Schußwaffen:

1. Vorderladerwaffen;
2. von den Hinterladerwaffen:
   a) Gewehrmodelle bis zum Konstruktionsjahr 1870 einschließlich,
   b) Zimmerstutzen,
   c) Flobertgewehre (Teschings) mit gezogenem Laufe mit einem Kaliber von 6 mm und darunter sowie Flobertgewehre mit nicht gezogenem Laufe mit einem Kaliber von 9 mm und darunter;
3. Waffen der im § 20 Nr. 2 und 3 dieser Verordnung bezeichneten Art.

(2) Eines Waffenscheins bedarf es ferner nicht zum Führen von Selbstschuß- und von Viehbetäubungsapparaten.

§ 23

(1) Den Waffenerwerbschein und den Waffenschein stellt die Kreispolizeibehörde aus, in deren Bezirk der Antragsteller seinen Wohnsitz oder dauernden Aufenthalt hat. In dringenden Fällen kann auch die Kreispolizeibehörde, in deren Bezirk sich der Antragsteller nur vorübergehend aufhält, den Schein ausstellen; diese hat von der Ausstellung die Kreispolizeibehörde, in deren Bezirk der Antragsteller seinen Wohnsitz oder dauernden Aufenthalt hat, zu benachrichtigen.

(2) Hat der Antragsteller seinen Wohnsitz oder dauernden Aufenthalt nicht innerhalb des Deutschen Reichs, so ist die Kreispolizeibehörde zuständig, in deren Bezirk der Aufenthalts- oder der Einreiseort liegt.

(3) In den Fällen des Abs. 1 Satz 2 und des Abs. 2 ist die Geltungsdauer des Scheines auf höchstens drei Monate festzusetzen.

§ 24

Der Waffenerwerbschein und der Waffenschein sind nach den aus den Anlagen I und II ersichtlichen Mustern auszustellen.

§ 25

(1) Wer Faustfeuerwaffen auf Grund eines Waffenerwerbscheins einem anderen überläßt, hat auf dem Scheine die Waffen nach Zahl, Art, aufgedruckter Firma oder Warenzeichen und Herstellungsnummer sowie das Datum der Überlassung mit Tinte oder Tintenstift zu vermerken.

(2) Der Erwerbschein ist dem Erwerber zurückzugeben, wenn die Zahl, auf die er lautet, noch nicht erreicht ist. Andernfalls hat der Überlasser den Erwerbschein binnen zwei Wochen der Kreispolizeibehörde einzureichen, in deren Bezirk er seinen Wohnsitz hat. Gehört er zu den in den §§ 3, 7 des Gesetzes bezeichneten Gewerbetreibenden, so hat er die Erwerbscheine gesammelt am Ende jedes Kalendermonats der Kreispolizeibehörde einzureichen, in deren Bezirk er seine gewerbliche Niederlassung hat.

(3) Ebenso ist mit Bescheinigungen zu verfahren, die nach § 20 des Gesetzes ausgestellt sind und zum Erwerb einer Faustfeuerwaffe berechtigen.

§ 26

Die Bescheinigungen nach § 12 Nr. 6 und § 24 Abs. 2 des Gesetzes stellt für die im § 3 des Gesetzes bezeichneten Gewerbetreibenden die höhere Verwaltungsbehörde (§ 5 dieser Verordnung), für die im § 7 des Gesetzes bezeichneten Gewerbetreibenden die Kreispolizeibehörde (§ 6 dieser Verordnung) aus.

§ 27

Ausnahmen nach § 13 Abs. 2 des Gesetzes bewilligt die Kreispolizeibehörde, in deren Bezirk der Jugendliche seinen Wohnsitz oder dauernden Aufenthalt hat. Hält er sich nur vorübergehend innerhalb des Deutschen Reichs auf, so bewilligt die Ausnahme die Kreispolizeibehörde, in deren Bezirk er sich aufhält.

§ 28

Ausnahmen nach § 15 Abs. 3 des Gesetzes bewilligt die höhere Verwaltungsbehörde, in deren Bezirk der Antragsteller seinen Wohnsitz oder dauernden Aufenthalt hat. Hält er sich nur vorübergehend innerhalb des Deutschen Reichs auf, so bewilligt die Ausnahme die höhere Verwaltungsbehörde, in deren Bezirk er sich aufhält.

§ 29

(1) Die landesrechtlichen Gebühren für die Ausstellung von Waffenerwerbscheinen und Waffenscheinen dürfen 3 Reichsmark für den Schein nicht übersteigen.

(2) Für Doppel dürfen nur Schreibgebühren erhoben werden.

§ 30

Zum Widerruf und zur Einziehung des Waffenerwerbscheins und des Waffenscheins ist die Kreispolizeibehörde zuständig, in deren Bezirk der Inhaber des Scheines seinen Wohnsitz oder dauernden Aufenthalt hat. Hält er sich nur vorübergehend innerhalb des Deutschen Reichs auf, so ist die Kreispolizeibehörde zuständig, in deren Bezirk er sich aufhält.

§ 31

Bescheinigungen nach § 20 des Gesetzes sind gesondert

1. für das Führen einer einzelnen Schußwaffe,
2. für den Erwerb einer einzelnen Faustfeuerwaffe

auszustellen.

§ 32

Jagdwaffen im Sinne des § 21 des Gesetzes sind Schußwaffen, die zur Verwendung bei der Jagd auf jagdbare Tiere bestimmt sind und hierbei üblicherweise verwendet werden.

§ 33

Zum Erlaß eines Verbots nach § 23 Abs. 1 des Gesetzes sowie zur Einziehung von Waffen und Munition nach § 23 Abs. 2 des Gesetzes ist die Kreispolizeibehörde zuständig, in deren Bezirk die Person, gegen die sich das Verbot richtet, ihren Wohnsitz oder dauernden Aufenthalt hat.

§ 34

(1) Die Erlaubnis zur Einfuhr gemäß § 24 des Gesetzes erteilt die Kreispolizeibehörde, in deren Bezirk der Einführende seinen Wohnsitz oder Aufenthalt hat oder in deren Bezirk sein Einreiseort liegt.

(2) Die Zollbehörde vermerkt auf der Bescheinigung, durch die die Erlaubnis erteilt ist, die Einfuhr und gibt die Bescheinigung sodann an die Polizeibehörde, die sie ausgestellt hat, zurück.

(3) Einer Erlaubnis zur Einfuhr nach § 24 des Gesetzes bedarf es außer in den im § 24 Abs. 2 des Gesetzes bezeichneten Fällen nicht:

1. für deutsche Staatsangehörige hinsichtlich solcher Schußwaffen und Munition, mit denen sie aus dem Ausland in das Inland wieder einreisen;
2. für Mitglieder ausländischer Schießsportverbände, die zu Schießsportveranstaltungen des Deutschen Reichsbundes für Leibesübungen oder des Deutschen Schützenverbandes einreisen, hinsichtlich der von ihnen zwecks Teilnahme an diesen Veranstaltungen mitgeführten Schußwaffen und Munition;
3. für Personen, die ihren Wohnsitz nicht im Reichsgebiet haben, für die von ihnen mitgeführten Jagdwaffen und Munition, deren Einfuhr von einer deutschen Vertretung im Ausland (Botschaft, Gesandtschaft oder Berufskonsulat) durch Unbedenklichkeitserklärung zugelassen wird.

§ 35

(1) Ausnahmen für die Herstellung, den Handel und den Besitz der im § 25 des Gesetzes bezeichneten Schußwaffen, Vorrichtungen und Patronen zur Ausfuhr bewilligt die höhere Verwaltungsbehörde, in deren Bezirk der Antragsteller seine gewerbliche Niederlassung hat.

(2) Schußwaffen, Vorrichtungen und Patronen, die von Behörden des Reichs oder der Länder oder von der Reichsbank zu dienstlichen Zwecken benötigt werden, fallen nicht unter das Verbot des § 25 Abs. 1 des Gesetzes.

§ 36

In der Verordnung über ein vorübergehendes Verbot der Einfuhr von Faustfeuerwaffen vom 12. Juni 1933 (Reichsgesetzbl. I S. 367) erhält Abs. 2 folgende Fassung:

„Ausnahmen im Einzelfalle sind unter den Voraussetzungen des § 24 Abs. 1 des Waffengesetzes vom 18. März 1938 (Reichsgesetzbl. I S. 265) zulässig.“

Berlin, den 19. März 1938.

Der Reichsminister des Innern

Frick

(Vorderseite)

Anlage I

(Zum § 24 der Verordnung)

Waffenerwerbschein Nr. ....

Gültig auf ein Jahr

....

wohnhaft ....

wird hierdurch die Erlaubnis zum Erwerbe von ....

.... erteilt.

(Stempel)

......................................, den .... 19 ....
(Ort)

....
(Dienststelle)

(Rückseite)

Es wurde überlassen

Lfde. Nr.	Datum	Zahl	Art	Aufgedruckte Firma oder Warenzeichen	Her-stellungs-nummer	Name, Wohnort und Wohnung des Überlassers
1	2	3	4	5	6	7

Anlage II

(Zum § 24 der Verordnung)

Platz für Lichtbild	**Waffenschein Nr.** ....
	Gültig auf drei Jahre
	....
	wohnhaft in ....
	geboren am .... in ....
	wird hierdurch die Erlaubnis zum Führen ....
	....
....	innerhalb des Deutschen Reichs ....
	.... erteilt.
	........................, den .... 19...... (Ort)
(Eigenhändige Unterschrift des Inhabers)	(Stempel) .... (Dienststelle)

Ausführungsbestimmungen

zu § 9 Abs. 2 Satz 2 und § 11 Satz 2 der Verordnung zur Durchführung des Waffengesetzes.

Vom 21. März 1938.

Auf Grund des § 9 Abs. 2 Satz 2 und des § 11 Satz 2 der Verordnung zur Durchführung des Waffengesetzes vom 19. März 1938 (Reichsgesetzbl. I S. 270) wird im Einvernehmen mit dem Reichsminister des Innern folgendes bestimmt:

§ 1

(1) Die Stelle, vor der die sachliche Eignung für das Herstellungs- oder das Handelsgewerbe im Sinne der §§ 9 Abs. 2 und 11 der Durchführungsverordnung vom 19. März 1938 (vgl. auch § 3 Abs. 2 bis 5 und § 7 des Gesetzes) nachzuweisen ist, ist ein von der Industrie- und Handelskammer zu bestimmender Sachverständiger, der durch langjährige Beschäftigung mit der Herstellung von Waffen und Munition vertraut sein muß. Der Sachverständige braucht nicht Mitglied der Industrie- und Handelskammer zu sein. Die Ernennung des Sachverständigen ist von der Industrie- und Handelskammer in geeigneter Weise bekanntzumachen.

(2) Die fachliche Eignung für die Herstellung von Schießpulver jeder Art ist durch eine Prüfung vor dem zuständigen Gewerbeaufsichtsamt nachzuweisen.

§ 2

Es findet nur eine mündliche Prüfung statt. Der Bewerber hat darin ausreichende Kenntnisse über die Art, Konstruktion und Handhabung der gebräuchlichsten Schußwaffen und über die Behandlung und Verwendung der gebräuchlichsten Munition nachzuweisen.

§ 3

Über das Ergebnis der Prüfung (§ 2) hat der Sachverständige eine Bescheinigung zu erteilen. Die Industrie- und Handelskammer kann zur Deckung der Kosten von dem Bewerber eine Gebühr bis zu 5 Reichsmark erheben.

Berlin, den 21. März 1938.

Der Reichswirtschaftsminister

In Vertretung

Brinkmann

Herausgegeben vom Reichsministerium des Innern. — Gedruckt in der Reichsdruckerei, Berlin.

Law Gazette of the Reich

Division I

1938	Issued in Berlin, March 21, 1938	No. 31

Firearms Act

March 18, 1938

The government of the Reich has passed the following Act, announced herewith:

Part I

General

§1

(1) In the context of this Act, firearms are weapons which operate on the principle of a solid body being forced through a barrel by means of gas or air pressure.

(2) In the context of this Act, ammunition includes ready-to-use ammunition for firearms as well as gunpowder of all kinds.

(3) Finished or prefabricated essential components of firearms or ammunition are equivalent to finished firearms or finished ammunition.

§2

In the context of this Act, cutting or thrusting weapons are weapons which are by their nature intended to inflict injury through cutting, thrusting or stabbing.

Part II

Manufacture of Firearms and Ammunition

§3

(1) Anyone who manufactures, modifies or repairs firearms or ammunition on a professional basis must obtain a permit. The refilling of cartridge cases is equivalent to the manufacture of ammunition.

(2) A permit may only be issued if the applicant is a German citizen with a fixed place of residence within the territory of the Reich.

(3) The Reich Minister of Domestic Affairs, in agreement with the Reich Ministers concerned, may admit of exceptions to the provisions of Section 2.

(4) Further, a permit may only be issued if the applicant and the persons participating in the technical direction of his business evidence the personal trustworthiness requisite for the conduct of such business, and if the applicant or the person participating in the technical direction of his trade possesses the requisite professional qualifications.

(5) A permit may not be issued if the applicant and the persons participating in the technical direction of his business, or one of the above, is a Jew.

§4

(1) On issuing a permit, a period of up to one year may be set within which operation must be begun, in default of which the permit expires. If no period is specified, the permit expires if operation is not begun within one year from the date of issue. Deadlines may be extended if good reason exists for doing so.

(2) Further, the permit expires if the manufacturer has not practised his craft for one year without having been granted an extension beyond that period, within which operations must be resumed. This period may be no more than one year; it may be extended if good reason exists for doing so.

(3) The manufacturer must file a written advisory notice within one week of commencing or ceasing operations.

§5

(1) The manufacturer's permit is to be revoked if the manufacturer or the business manager as a person no longer fulfills the requirements for the issuance of the permit.

(2) If a permit is to be revoked, the conduct of operations may be temporarily suspended with immediate effect. This measure ceases to be in force if a request for revocation is not submitted within one week to the proper authorities, which decide on the temporary suspension of the permit; this decision may not be appealed.

§6

If the permit has been denied or revoked, a new permit may be issued within the period of two years only if special circumstances justify such a measure.

Part III
Dealing in Weapons and Ammunition

§7

(1) Anyone who, on a professional basis, purchases, offers for sale, or otherwise provides to others, either firearms or ammunition, or who, on a professional basis, acts as mediator in the purchase or provision of such items, or who, on a professional basis, offers his services to effect their purchase or provision, requires a permit to do so.

(2) The regulations set out in § 3 Sections 2 to 5 and §§ 4 to 6 apply as appropriate.

(3) A permit issued in accordance with § 3 Section 1 also includes in its scope the professional purchasing, selling or provision to others, of firearms and ammunition.

§8

A permit in accordance with § 7 may not be issued to junk dealers.

§9

(1) Dealing in firearms, ammunition, and cutting and thrusting weapons is prohibited:

1. to travelling vendors;

2. at festivals, events featuring shooting competitions, and fairs, with the exception of trade fairs.

(2) The selling and provision of ammunition required at shooting booths or ranges at shooting competitions is exempted from the regulation of Section 1 Clause 2.

§10

(1) Firearms which are sold or provided to others on a professional basis must be identified by the manufacturer's company name and with a production serial number.

(2) Firearms not identified by the name of a domestic manufacturer must be marked with the registered trademark of a domestic dealer, in addition to being identified with the data specified in Section 1.

Part IV
Purchase, Carrying, Ownership and Import of Weapons and Ammunition

§11

(1) Handguns may be provided or purchased only on submission of a Weapons Acquisition Permit.

(2) The Weapons Acquisition Permit is valid for one year from the date of issue.

(3) Section 1 does not apply to:

a) the provision of handguns at shooting booths or ranges licensed by the police, where the handguns are to be used on-site only;

b) the direct export of handguns out of the country;

c) the conveyance of handguns by persons who on a professional basis arrange or conduct the transport of goods, particularly by haulers, carriers, ocean shipping agents, the German Reich Postal Service, or the German Reich Railway;

d) acquisition by inheritance.

§12

A Weapons Acquisition Permit is not required for:

1. authorities of the Reich or the Lands [states], the Reich Railway, and Operation "Reichsautobahnen" [federal highways];

2. communities (community associations) whom the highest authorities of their Land have given permission to obtain weapons without a Weapons Acquisition Permit;

3. the departments of the National Socialist German Workers' Party and its subdivisions, as determined by the Führer's Second-in-Command;

4. the departments of the Anti-Aircraft Defense and the National Socialist Fliers' Corps, as determined by the Reich Minister of Aviation;

5. the departments of Technical Emergency Assistance, as determined by the Reich Minister of Domestic Affairs;

6. the manufacturers and dealers set out in §§ 3, 7 who are officially licensed;

7. holders of weapons permits and annual hunting licenses.

§13

(1) Firearms and ammunition as well as cutting and thrusting weapons may not be sold to minors under the age of 18.

(2) An appropriate government authority may admit of exceptions.

§14

(1) Anyone who carries a firearm on his person outside his place of residence, service, or business, or his fenced-in property must carry a Weapons Permit on his person. "Carrying a firearm" does not apply to firing ranges authorized by the police.

(2) Provided that its validity is not expressly restricted to a smaller area, the Weapons Permit is valid throughout the Reich proper. Its validity can be restricted to specify clearly defined occasions or areas.

(3) A Weapons Permit is valid for a period of three years from the date of issue, provided that a shorter period is not specified.

§15

(1) Weapons Acquisition Permits or Weapons Permits may only be issued to persons whose trustworthiness is not in question and who can prove a need for a permit.

(2) In particular, permits may not be issued to:

1. persons under the age of 18 years;

2. legally incapacitated or mentally inferior persons;

3. Gypsies or vagabond persons;

4. persons under mandatory police supervision or who have been relieved of their civil rights—for as long as these remain under mandatory police supervision or remain stripped of their civil rights;

5. persons convicted of treason or high treason, or with respect to whom known facts justify the assumption that they are engaged in activities hostile to the state;

6. persons who, for a deliberate assault on the life or well-being of others, for breach of the peace or for trespass, for resistance to the authority of the state, for a criminal offense or misdemeanor, for a criminal offence against property, for a hunting violation, or for a fishing violation, were legally sentenced to a term of imprisonment of more than two weeks, if three years have not yet passed since the term of imprisonment. Serving the sentence is equivalent to its lapse, its remission, or its commutation to a monetary fine; in this case, the three-year-period begins on the date of the sentence's lapse, remission, or commutation to a monetary fine. If the penalty is entirely or partially remitted after a period of probation, the probationary period is credited towards the three-year period.

(3) Exceptions to Section 2 Clauses 1 and 6 may be granted upon application.

§16

The issue of Weapons Acquisition Permits or Weapons Permits entails fees to be levied in accordance with specifics to be set out by the Enforcement Ordinance.

§17

The Weapons Acquisition Permit or Weapons Permit is to be revoked and confiscated if the prerequisites for its issue are not met, or are no longer met.

§18

With respect to the firearms provided to them in the line of duty, the following persons do not require Weapons Acquisition Permits or Weapons Permits:

1. members of the Wehrmacht;

2. police officers, including railway police officers, members of the railway security service, and members of the postal security service;

3. members of the SS Task Force and the SS Death's-Head Corps;

4. officials of the penal institutions of the Reich Department of Justice;

5. those officials of the Reich Department of Revenue who are employed in border supervision, border clearance, and customs investigation services;

6. those officials of Operation "Reichsautobahnen" whose duties include the monitoring of roads and highways;

7. those officials and employees serving in forest, field and game protection who have either sworn an oath of service or who, due to juridical stipulations, are bound by oath or are officially certified as authorities of forest, field and game protection, as well as fishery officials and the officially certified Supervisor of Fisheries.

§19

(1) Further, with respect to the firearms provided to them in the line of duty, the following persons do not require Weapons Acquisition Permits or Weapons Permits:

1. those persons in the service of the Reich, the Lands, the Bank of the Reich, and Operation "Reichsautobahnen," to whom the appropriate Reich or Land authorities, the Bank of the Reich, or the "Reichsautobahnen" have granted the right to bear firearms;

2. Unterführer of the National Socialist Workers' Party from the rank of Ortsgruppenleiter up, the SA, the SS, the National Socialist Motorized Corps from the rank of Sturmführer up, as well as the Hitler Youth from the rank of Bannführer up, to whom the Führer's Second-in-Command or an authority appointed by him have granted the right to bear firearms; also, the members of the SA guard group Feldherrnhalle, in such cases as the Führer decrees;

3. Führer of Technical Emergency Assistance to whom the Reich Minister of Domestic Affairs has granted the right to carry firearms;

4. members of the Anti-Aircraft Defense Service to whom the Reich Minister of Aviation or the agency determined by him has granted the right to carry firearms. The Reich Minister of Aviation and the Reich Minister of Domestic Affairs together decide to which groups of persons this right applies;

5. Führer of the National Socialist Fliers' Corps, from the ranks of Sturmführer and independent Truppführer up, as well as independent heads of schools to whom the Reich Minister of Aviation or the agency determined by him has granted the right to carry firearms.

(2) In these cases, the Weapons Permit is replaced by an appropriate certificate, to be issued to persons coming under Section 1 Nos. 1, 3 to 5 by their superior or supervisory department and to persons coming under Section 1 No. 2 by the Führer's Second-in-Command or by the agency determined by him.

§20

If firearms are not officially provided to persons coming under §§18, 19, or if weapons other than those officially supplied are required, the superior or supervisory department or, for persons coming under §19 Section 1 No. 2, the Führer's Second-in-Command or the agency determined by him, are authorized to issue certificates entitling these persons to purchase or carry a firearm.

§21

A hunting license authorizes its bearer to carry hunting weapons and handguns.

§22

(1) The acquisition of weapons of war is permitted only with the authorization of the Wehrmacht Supreme Command or the agencies determined by it.

(2) The term "weapons of war" refers to all equipment as defined by the regulations of November 6, 1935, governing the export and import of weapons of war (Law Gazette of the Reich I, p. 1337).

§23

(1) In individual cases, a person who has engaged in activities hostile to the state, or who may be expected to pose a danger to public safety, may be prohibited from acquiring, possessing and carrying firearms and ammunition as well as cutting and thrusting weapons.

(2) Weapons and ammunition in the possession of persons to whom this prohibition has been applied are to be confiscated without compensation.

§24

(1) Importing firearms and ammunition through customs requires a permit. This permit is to be denied if there are doubts as to the trustworthiness of the importer. The regulations of §15 Section 2, 3 and §17 apply analogously to the issuance and revocation of this permit.

(2) Section 1 does not apply to import by authorities of the Reich or the Lands, nor does it apply to manufacturers and dealers in accordance with §§3, 7, who are officially licensed.

(3) The regulations of November 6, 1935, regarding the export and import of weapons of war (Law Gazette of the Reich I, p. 1337) are not affected.

(4) In the customs and foreign trade zones, firearms and ammunition are governed by regulations to be issued jointly by the Reich Minister of Finance and the Reich Minister of Domestic Affairs.

§25

(1) Manufacture, trade, carrying, possession and import of the following are prohibited:

1. firearms specially designed to be folded, collapsed, shortened, or rapidly disassembled beyond the measure usual for hunting and sports purposes, or which are concealed in canes, umbrellas, piping or in similar ways;

2. firearms equipped with a device to silence the report of a shot, or with rifle spotlights; this ban also extends to these modifying devices in and of themselves;

3. cartridges of caliber .22, short, long, or long rifle (small caliber cartridges) with hollow-point bullets (bullets with pierced or notched tips).

(2) For export purposes, the manufacture, trade and possession of the firearms, devices and cartridges specified in Section 1 may be permitted.

Part V
Penal Laws

§26

(1) Anyone who

1. manufactures, modifies, repairs, acquires, offers for sale, makes available to others, possesses or imports weapons, ammunition or the devices described in §25 Section 1 No. 2, mediates in the acquisition or making available of such objects, or offers his services towards the end of their acquisition or making available, or who

2. carries firearms

in deliberate or negligent violation of the present law, will be penalized with up to three years' imprisonment and/or a monetary fine.

(2) Over and above this penalty, the weapons, ammunition or devices to which the punishable act in question relates may be confiscated regardless of whether they belong to the offender or not. If no specific individual/s can be prosecuted or convicted, confiscation may be carried out without these concomitants if the prerequisites for such a measure exist.

§27

(1) A monetary fine of up to one hundred and fifty Reichsmark or a term of imprisonment applies to anyone who

1. deliberately or through negligence fails to file, or to file in time, the written advisory notice required under §4 Section 3,

2. deliberately or through negligence violates the juridical stipulations for the enforcement or supplementation (§24 Section 4, §31) of the present Act.

(2) Anyone who deliberately violates the regulations set out in Section 1 No. 2 after having been twice previously convicted for deliberate or negligent violation of the same will be punished with a term of up to one year in prison and/or a monetary fine. This regulation does not apply if more than three years have passed since the last conviction prior to commission of the new offence.

Part VI
Final and Interim Regulations

§28

The manufacturing and trading enterprises specified in §§3, 7 are subject to the usual trading regulations insofar as no special regulations have been set out in the present Act.

§29

(1) Anyone who is already licensed to carry on any of the endeavors specified in §§ 3, 7 when the present law comes into force does not need to obtain a new permit. However, the prior license, issued in accordance with the Firearms and Ammunitions Act of April 12, 1928 (Law Gazette of the Reich I, p. 143) is to be revoked by March 31, 1939 if the prerequisites set out in §3 Sections 2 to 5 are not met at this time. Weapons manufacturers are not required to provide proof of their professional qualifications if, at the time the present law comes into force, they have practiced their craft for five years without interruption. Further, licenses for the trade in firearms and ammunition issued in accordance with §5 of the Firearms and Ammunitions Act may be revoked if there is no local requirement for maintaining this license.

(2) If a manufacturer or dealer has not required a permit to date because the firearms or ammunition in question did not come under the Firearms and Ammunitions Act of April 12,

1928, (Law Gazette of the Reich I, p. 143), then, if these firearms or ammunition are subject to the present Act, a permit such as required by §§3, 7 must be applied for within a period of one month after this law comes into force.

(3) If Section 2 applies, a criminal offence as detailed in §26 Section 1 No. 1 occurs if one month lapses following the coming into force of the present law, or, if a permit was applied for within this period, at the end of one month after this permit was definitely refused.

§30

(1) Firearms which do not bear the identifying markings stipulated in §10 may still be professionally sold or made available to others for the period of one year after this law comes into force, provided that their identifying markings meet the requirements set out in §9 of the Firearms and Ammunitions Act of April 12, 1928, (Law Gazette of the Reich I, p. 143) or if they were not addressed by these regulations.

(2) For firearms which were not addressed by the Firearms and Ammunitions Act of April 12, 1928, (Law Gazette of the Reich I, p. 143) and whose manufacturer can no longer be determined, has ceased to exist, or ceases to exist within one year after the present law comes into force, the identifying markings stipulated by §10 of the present Act may be substituted with identification consisting of the business name or registered trademark of a domestic dealer, inscribed on the firearm.

§31

The Reich Minister of Domestic Affairs will enact the juridical and administrative regulations required for the enforcement and supplementation of the present Act. He has the power to admit of exceptions to the present Act for certain kinds of weapons or ammunition.

§32

Farther-reaching restrictions issued by individual Lands to govern the manufacture, trading, acquisition, carrying or possession of cutting and thrusting weapons will cease to be in effect at most six months after the present law comes into force, except insofar as they pertain to Gypsies or vagabond persons.

§33

(1) The present law will come into force on April 1, 1938.

(2) At the same time, the following cease to be in force:

1. the Firearms and Ammunitions Act of April 12, 1928, (Law Gazette of the Reich I, p. 143);

2. the regulations for the implementation of the Firearms and Ammunitions Act, of July 13, 1928, (Law Gazette of the Reich I, p. 198), version of the decree of June 2, 1932, (Law Gazette of the Reich I, p. 253);

3. the Weapons Abuse Act of March 28, 1931, (Law Gazette of the Reich I, p. 77), version of §10 of the Reich President's decree regarding the Preservation of Domestic Order, December 19, 1932, (Law Gazette of the Reich I, p. 548);

4. Chapter I (Measures against Weapons Abuse) of Part 8 of the Reich President's Fourth Decree regarding the Safeguarding of the Economy and Finances and the Preservation of Domestic Order, December 8, 1931, (Law Gazette of the Reich I, pp. 699, 742);

5. §56 Section 2 Clause 8 of the Trading Regulations.

(3) The right to introduce this Act in Austria is reserved.

Berlin, March 18, 1938

Führer and Chancellor of the Reich
Adolf Hitler

Reich Minister of Domestic Affairs
Frick

Ordinance for the Enforcement of the Firearms Act

March 19, 1938

In accordance with §31 of the Firearms Act of March 18, 1938, (Law Gazette of the Reich I, p. 265), the following is decreed:

Part I

General

§1

(1) In the context of this Ordinance, the "higher administrative authorities" are: in Prussia and Bavaria, the Chairman of the Regional Council (in Berlin, the Chief of Police); in Saxony, the District Captain; in the Saarland, the Reich Commissioner for the Saarland; and otherwise, the highest authority of a Land.

(2) In the context of this Ordinance, the district police authorities are: the state police in communities under state police administration; elsewhere,

in city districts : the Mayor,

in county districts : in Prussia, the District Councillor; in the other Lands, the corresponding authorities.

§2

(1) Decisions made by the administrative authorities on the basis of the Firearms Act may be appealed within two weeks. Appeals may be addressed only to the immediately superior administrative authorities, whose decision is then final.

(2) Objections to decisions made by the Berlin Chief of Police in his capacity as local or district police authority may be registered as formal protest, not as appeal. The Chief of Police himself, his general representative, or a department chief of the police headquarters in Berlin may decide on the protest.

§3

(1) In the context of §1 Section 3 of the Act, the following are deemed to be essential components:

a) for firearms—barrel, lock, revolving breech;

b) for ammunition—case, bullet.

(2) In the context of §1 Section 3 of the Act, prefabricated essential components are only such objects, described in Section 1, which are in a sufficiently advanced state of manufacture that they can be finished, and used in the assembly of ready-to-use firearms or ready-to-use ammunition, without any special tools or machinery.

§4

Weapons operating on the principle of compressed air, and with a caliber of 7 mm and less, are not subject to the regulations of the Act, with the exception of §§9, 24 and 25.

Part II

Manufacture of Firearms and Ammunition, and Dealing in Such Objects

§5

Issuing and revoking a manufacturer's permit (§3 of the Act) is the responsibility of the higher administrative authorities in whose district the manufacturer has established his facilities.

§6

Issuing and revoking a dealership permit (§ 7 of the Act) is the responsibility of the district police authorities in whose district the dealer has established his facilities.

§7

Manufacturing and dealership permits may be restricted to specific kinds of firearms and ammunition.

§8

(1) The personal trustworthiness required for persons engaging in manufacture or dealing (§3 Section 4, §7 Section 2 of the Act) is to be ascertained through an examination with attention paid to the applicant's and the business managers' entire past histories.

(2) The mandatory personal trustworthiness is lacking particularly in persons who:

1. are not legally capable of contracting or whose capability to contract is restricted;

2. are under mandatory police supervision or who have been relieved of their civil rights—for as long as they remain under mandatory police supervision or remain stripped of their civil rights;

3. have been convicted of treason or high treason, or with respect to whom known facts justify the assumption that they are engaged in activities hostile to the state;

4. for a deliberate assault on the life or well-being of others, for breach of the peace or for trespass, for resistance to the authority of the state, for a criminal offence or misdemeanor, for a criminal offence motivated by a desire for material gain or directed against property, or for a hunting violation, were legally sentenced to a term of imprisonment of at least three months, if three years have not yet passed since the term of imprisonment. Serving the sentence is equivalent to its lapse, its remission, or its commutation to a monetary fine; in this case, the three-year period begins on the date of the sentence's lapse, remission, or commutation to a monetary fine. If the penalty is entirely or partially remitted after a period of probation, the probationary period is credited towards the three-year period.

§9

(1) Professional qualifications for manufacture (§3 Section 4 of the Act) are held only by such persons who either have passed the examination for master craftsman's diploma for the craft practised, or for a related craft, or who are authorized to instruct apprentices in one of these crafts. Examinations recognized under §133 Section 10 of the Trading Regulations are equivalent to the examination for master craftsman's diploma. The German Chamber of Crafts and Trade Convention decides which crafts are considered to be related in the context of this Ordinance.

(2) Professional qualifications for manufacture are further held by such persons who can prove professionally qualified status through the completion of relevant studies at a post-secondary institution or a state-accredited technical college, or in person before an authority to be determined by the Chamber of Commerce. The Reich Minister of Economic Affairs and the Reich Minister of Domestic Affairs will jointly decide on details of the professional requirements and the examination procedure.

§10

Foreign legal entities (corporate bodies) and legal entities whose capital is largely in foreign hands may not receive permission to engage in manufacture or dealership.

§11

Professional qualifications for dealership (§7 Section 2 of the Act) are held only by such persons who have either, for a period of at least three years, been the proprietor of a place of business where firearms and ammunition were sold, or who were employed as salesperson, assistant or apprentice for a period of at least three years, or who can prove professional qualifications before an authority to be determined by the Chamber of Commerce. The Reich

Minister of Economic Affairs and the Reich Minister of Domestic Affairs will jointly decide on details of the professional requirements and the examination procedure.

§12

Commencement or conclusion of business (§4 Section 3 of the Act) must be reported by a manufacturing firm to the higher administrative authorities and by a dealership to the district police authorities in whose district the manufacturer's or dealer's facilities are established.

§13

Permission to conduct manufacturing or trading activities is to be revoked (§§ 5, 7 Section 2 of the Act) if, at the time of issuing the permit, the issuing authorities were not aware that one of the reasons for denial set out in §3 Section 2 to 5 of the Act or in §8 Section 2 of this Ordinance existed, or if one of these reasons for denial occurred subsequently. In the case of loss or diminution of the capability to contract (§8 Section 2 No. 1 of this Ordinance), the permit is to be revoked only if no acting representative is brought in, in accordance with §45 of the Trading Regulations.

§14

Temporary denial of permission to carry on the business in question (§5 Section 2 of the Act) falls within the jurisdiction of the district police authorities in the case of manufacturing firms, the local police authorities in the case of dealerships; these authorities are those in whose district the manufacturer's or dealer's facilities are established.

§15

(1) Anyone who manufactures firearms on a professional basis must keep a Weapons Register showing the whereabouts of the firearms. The Weapons Register is to be set up as follows:

Serial No.	Date	Number	Make, Model	Name of Firm	Manufacturing No.	Name, Address of Purchaser
1	2	3	4	5	6	7

(2) Weapons of war are to be registered in a separate Weapons Register.

§16

(1) Anyone who, on a professional basis, purchases handguns, offers such for sale or otherwise provides such to others, or who, on a professional basis, acts as mediator in the purchase or provision of such items, must keep a Weapons Dealership Register showing the origins and whereabouts of the handguns. The Weapons Dealership Register is to be set up as follows:

Serial No.	Date	Number	Make, Model	Name of Firm or Trademark	Manufacturing No.	Name and Address of Supplier
1	2	3	4	5	6	7

(Left Side) **Incoming**

Serial No.	Date	Number	Make, Model	Name of Firm or Trademark	Manufacturing No.	Purchaser's Name, Address	Proof of Right to Purchase
8	9	10	11	12	13	14	15

(Right Side) **Outgoing**

(2) It is the seller's responsibility to make sure that the purchaser is authorized to acquire handguns. For this purpose, he must request the presentation of a Weapons Acquisition Permit, Weapons Permit or annual hunting license and record the kind, date and number of the permit in column 15 of the Weapons Dealership Register. If the purchaser is authorized to acquire handguns without a Weapons Acquisition Permit, then this must also be recorded in column 15 (e.g., Reich authority, weapons dealer).

§17

In cases of professional mediation of purchase or the provision of handguns, the Weapons Dealership Register (§16) is to be set up as follows:

Serial No.	Date	Number	Make, Model	Name and Address of Supplier	Name and Address of Purchaser
1	2	3	4	5	6

§18

(1) Weapons Registers and Weapons Dealership Registers (§§15 to 17) must be permanently bound and marked with consecutive page numbers. Prior to being used, the local police authorities must certify the number of pages contained in it. Entries in the register, once made, may neither be erased nor rendered illegible. All entries must be made in German, and written in ink or ink pencil. On December 31st of each year, as well as on transfer or closing of the business, the register must be dated and signed in such a way that later and additional entries cannot be made. Within one month after the start of the new calendar year or after transfer of the business, the book must be presented to the local police authorities for verification of closure. Stock remaining at the date of closure must be carried forward before new entries are made. The book is to be kept up-to-date at all times and to be made available, together with all required documentation, for inspection by the police or its representatives upon request.

(2) The dealer must retain the book for a period of ten years from the date of the last entry made therein. If the dealer closes his business, he must submit his registers to the local police authorities for safekeeping.

(3) The regulations set out in Sections 1 and 2 also go for the Weapons Register for weapons of war, with the proviso that the function of the local police authorities is carried out by a Section of the Wehrmacht, to be specified by the Wehrmacht Supreme Command.

§19

(1) In the context of §10 of the Act, "manufacturer" also includes anyone in Germany who professionally assembles firearms from parts manufactured by other domestic facilities.

(2) If firearms are assembled in Germany proper from parts produced by foreign manufacturers, the weapons must bear the company name and manufacturing number of the foreign manufacturer who manufactured the gun barrel.

(3) The following are exempted from §10 of the Act:

1. muzzle-loading guns;
2. rifles manufactured prior to and including the year 1870;
3. blank guns (weapons which cannot fire anything other than blank cartridges);
4. gas, sedation and stun weapons (weapons intended for use with gas, sedation and stun cartridges), with a caliber of 12 mm or less, if they have been specially designed to make the effective firing of bullet or shot cartridges impossible;
5. set-gun or spring-gun devices;
6. devices with which to sedate livestock.

Part III
Purchase, Carrying, Ownership and Import of Weapons and Ammunition

§20

Weapons Acquisition Permits are not required for providing or for acquiring the following handguns:

1. muzzle-loading pistols or revolvers;
2. blank guns (weapons which cannot fire anything other than blank cartridges);
3. gas, sedation and stun weapons (weapons intended for use with gas, sedation and stun cartridges), with a caliber of 12 mm or less, if they have been specially designed to make the effective firing of bullet or shot cartridges impossible.

§21

In accordance with §11 Section 3 Part b of the Act, a Weapons Acquisition Permit need not be submitted for the direct export of handguns out of the country. In the context of this regulation, the following are also considered to be "out of the country":

1. the customs zones, with the exception of Helgoland and the customs zones of Baden;
2. the foreign trade zones.

§22

(1) No Weapons Permit is required to carry the following firearms:

1. muzzle-loading weapons;
2. the following breech-loading weapons:
   a) rifles manufactured prior to and including the year 1870;
   b) saloon rifles;
   c) Flobert rifles [i.e., low-power, "indoor" target guns] with rifled barrels of 6 mm caliber and less, as well as those with non-rifled barrels of 9 mm caliber and less;
   d) weapons of the kinds specified in §20 No. 2 and 3 of this Ordinance.

(2) Further, no Weapons Permit is required to carry set-gun or spring-gun devices and devices for sedating livestock.

§23

(1) Weapons Acquisition Permits and Weapons Permits are issued by the district police authorities in whose district the applicant permanently resides. In urgent cases, the district police authorities in whose district the applicant is only temporarily resident may also issue permits; these police authorities must inform the district police authorities in whose district the applicant permanently resides that the permit has been issued.

(2) If the applicant's residence or fixed address is not located within the German Reich, issuing the permit is the responsibility of the district police authorities in whose district the applicant's place of residence or entry is located.

(3) In the cases outlined in Section 1 Clause 2 and Section 2, the permit is to be validated for a maximum duration of three months.

§24

The Weapons Acquisition Permits and the Weapons Permits are to be set up as shown in Enclosures I and II, attached.

§25

(1) Anyone who, on the authority of a Weapons Acquisition Permit, hands a handgun over to another person, must record on the permit, in ink or ink pencil, the number, make/model, manufacturer's firm or trademark, and manufacturing number of the handguns, as well as the date on which the handguns were transferred.

(2) The Acquisitions Permit is to be returned to the purchaser if the number of weapons for which it is valid has not yet been reached. Otherwise, the seller must, within two weeks, hand

the Acquisitions Permit in to the district police authorities in whose district he resides. If the seller is among the professionals specified in §§3, 7 of the Act, then he is to collect and retain all Acquisitions Permits and hand them in at the end of each calendar month to the district police authorities in whose district his place of business is located.

(3) The same process of permit collection and surrender applies to permits issued in accordance with §20 of the Act, which authorize the acquisition of a handgun.

§26

Licenses in accordance with §12 No. 6 and §24 Section 2 of the Act are issued by: for professionals specified in §3 of the Act, the higher administrative authorities (§5 of this Ordinance); for professionals specified in §7 of the Act, the district police authorities (§6 of this Ordinance).

§27

Exceptions as specified in §13 Section 2 of the Act are authorized by the district police authorities in whose district the minor is permanently resident. If he is only temporarily resident in the German Reich, the exception is authorized by the district police authorities in whose district he is resident.

§28

Exceptions as specified in §15 Section 3 of the Act are authorized by the higher administrative authorities in whose district the applicant is permanently resident. If he is only temporarily resident in the German Reich, the exception is authorized by the higher administrative authorities in whose district he is resident.

§29

(1) The fees levied by a Land for the issuing of Weapons Acquisition Permits and Weapons Permits may not exceed 3 Reichsmark.

(2) For duplicates, only writing fees may be levied.

§30

Revocation and confiscation of Weapons Acquisition Permits and Weapons Permits is the responsibility of the district police authorities in whose district the holder of the permit is permanently resident. If he is only temporarily resident in the German Reich, this is the responsibility of the district police authorities in whose district he is resident.

§31

Licenses as specified in §20 of the Act are to be issued separately for:

1. possession of a single firearm;
2. acquisition of a single handgun.

§32

Hunting weapons as specified in § 21 of the Act are firearms intended for use, and commonly used, in hunting animals which may legally be hunted.

§33

Enacting a prohibition in accordance with § 23 Section 1 of the Act, as well as the confiscation of weapons and ammunition in accordance with §23 Section 2 of the Act, is the responsibility of the district police authorities in whose district the person to whom this prohibition has been applied permanently resides.

§34

(1) A license to import in accordance with §24 of the Act is issued by the district police authorities in whose district the importer is permanently resident or in whose district his place of entry is located.

(2) The customs authorities record the importation on the license authorizing such import and return the license to the police authorities who issued it.

(3) Except in the cases specified in §24 Section 2 of the Act, the following do not require a license to import in accordance with §24 of the Act:

1. German citizens—with respect to firearms and ammunition with which they are re-entering Germany proper from a foreign country;

2. members of foreign rifle clubs who are entering Germany to participate in shooting events held by the German Reich Association for Physical Education or the German Rifle Club—with respect to the firearms and ammunition brought with them for purposes of participation in these events;

3. persons who are not permanently resident in the German Reich—with respect to hunting weapons and ammunition whose importation has been sanctioned by a foreign representative of Germany (embassy, legation, or consulate).

§35

(1) Exceptions pertaining to the export-bound manufacture, trading and possession of the firearms, devices or cartridges specified in §25 of the Act are granted by the higher administrative authorities in whose district the applicant's business is located.

(2) Firearms, devices and cartridges required in the line of duty by authorities of the Reich or the Lands or by the Reichsbank are exempted from the ban placed on them by §25 Section 1 of the Act.

§36

The Ordinance of June 12, 1933, regarding a temporary ban on the importation of handguns (Law Gazette of the Reich I, p. 367), Section 2, is amended as follows:

"Individual exceptions may be permitted in accordance with §24 Section 1 of the Firearms Act of March 18, 1938, (Law Gazette of the Reich I, p. 265)."

Berlin, March 19, 1938

Reich Minister of Domestic Affairs
Frick

Enclosure I
(cf. §24 of the Enforcement Ordinance)

Front Side

Weapons Acquisition Permit No.______

Valid for one year

____

resident in ____

is hereby authorized to acquire ______________________________

____.

(City or town) ____________________, (date) ________ 19 __.

Stamp

____
(Branch Office)

Back Side

Firearms Acquired						
Serial No.	Date	Number	Make, Model	Name of Firm or Trademark	Manufacturing No.	Name and Address of Supplier
1	2	3	4	5	6	7

Enclosure II
(cf. §24 of the Enforcement Ordinance)

<table>
<tr><td>Photograph</td><td>

Weapons Permit No. ________

Valid for three years

____
resident in ______________________
born on ____________ in ____________
is hereby authorized to carry ______________
____
within the boundaries of the German Reich.

(City or town)________________, (date) ________ 19__.
</td></tr>
<tr><td>______________
(Signature of Bearer)</td><td>Stamp
____
(Branch Office)</td></tr>
</table>

Regulations for the Implementation of §9 Section 2 Clause 2 and §11 Clause 2 of the Ordinance for the Enforcement of the Firearms Act

March 21, 1938

On the basis of §9 Section 2 Clause 2 and §11 Clause 2 of the Ordinance for the Enforcement of the Firearms Act of March 19, 1938, (Law Gazette of the Reich I, p. 270), the following is decreed jointly with the Reich Minister of Domestic Affairs:

§1

(1) The authority before whom professional qualifications for engaging in manufacture or dealership are to be proven in accordance with §9 Section 2 and §11 of the Ordinance for the Enforcement of the Firearms Act of March 19, 1938, (cf. also §3 Section 2 to 5 and §7 of the Act) is a subject expert to be appointed by the Chamber of Commerce, who must be familiar with the manufacture of weapons and ammunition through many years' experience. This subject expert need not be a member of the Chamber of Commerce. The appointment of this subject expert will be publicized in an appropriate manner by the Chamber of Commerce.

(2) Professional qualifications for the manufacture of gunpowder of all kinds are to be proven at an examination held by the appropriate Factory Inspectorate.

§2

The examination will be verbal only. The applicant must prove sufficient knowledge of the kinds, construction and use of the most common firearms and of the handling and use of the most commonly used ammunition.

§3

The subject expert will issue a certificate reflecting the results of the examination (§2). To recover the costs involved, the Chamber of Commerce may levy a fee of up to 5 Reichsmark, payable by the applicant.

Berlin, March 21, 1938

Reich Minister of Economic Affairs
(on behalf of)
Brinkmann

Published by the Reich Ministry of Domestic Affairs. — Printed in the Reich Printing Office, Berlin.